Evernote

A Success Manual for College Students

Stan Skrabut, Ed.D.

EVERNOTE, the Evernote Elephant logo and REMEMBER EVERYTHING are trademarks of Evernote Corporation and used under a license.

Paperback ISBN: 979-8-9855537-0-3

eBook ISBN: 979-8-9855537-1-0

Contents

Acknowledgments

I am deeply grateful for all the support I received while writing this book. Writing a book requires a team effort. It would not have been possible without these wonderful people.

First, a huge thank you goes out to my wife and partner, Bernadette van der Vliet. She has reviewed countless drafts and provided invaluable design recommendations throughout this project. Each recommendation has helped make each version better. Her design skills have gone to the creation of a wonderful cover and countless marketing images. She continues to make me look good. I can't thank her enough.

Second, when it comes to editing, I repeatedly put my trust into Steve Miller. Every time, I give Steve a draft of my work, he returns it significantly better. I appreciate not only his editing skill but his patience of dealing with me.

Third, I can't thank my beta readers enough. This enthusiastic group of people provided me with valuable feedback regarding this book. Many of their suggestions made it into this final version. Their recommendations certainly took this project to the next level. Thank you, Becky Park, Jaclyn Quamo, Kelly Rys, Kim Stahl, and Bernadette van der Vliet. Thank you.

Introduction

I've been using Evernote since the end of 2010. One of my first notes was a syllabus for one of my graduate classes. I saw the potential of Evernote for students at once. From that moment forward, I started to use Evernote to capture documents, notes, and images related to my classes. It became my digital notebook.

The more I used Evernote, the more I recognized its power. I could combine notes and enhance them by adding text, audio, images, documents, and much more. I could search through Evernote to find my search query highlighted on pictures of slides and whiteboards. I had only one regret. I regret that I did not discover Evernote earlier in my academic career.

Evernote has served me well past my graduation. It has aided me in my professional life as well as my personal life. I have used it to take conference notes, meeting notes, and training notes. I have used it to move on two separate occasions. It is my digital brain.

Why This Book?

I wrote this book for college students who want to be more successful. I have been in higher education for over twenty years working as an instructional technologist. I am now at my fourth institution. Throughout my experiences, I have watched many students struggle with organization and recall. Evernote can help with both issues. This book is a manual for using Evernote, using Evernote as a college student, and being a better college student.

Disclaimer

Evernote continues to improve its applications and business model. As I release this manual, I am using Evernote version 10.21.5 for Windows. I had to do a complete rewrite of this manual since I started it because Evernote had a major release that changed the functionality.

In spite of my care and best attempt, you can expect that instructions and images will begin to differ over time. That is the nature of progress. Fortunately, Evernote keeps its help site current.

Evernote Version

Evernote has three plans (Learn more at https://evernote.com/compare-plans):

- Free

- Personal (The plan I am using)

- Professional

You can do many of the things I write about in this manual with the free plan. I recommend that you start with the free plan to get the feel of Evernote. You can load and sync Evernote on two of your devices. You should use the computer application or the web application and a mobile device to get started. While you can switch out which devices you use, you can only switch out a device twice a month.

As a college student, you can get 50% off a one-year subscription to Evernote Personal. You can access this discount at https://evernote.com/students.

How to Use This Manual

The book is meant to be read in order because each chapter builds on the previous one. However, you can also jump to a chapter that helps you solve an immediate question as you work with Evernote. I encourage you to create an account with Evernote and try the different strategies that I provide you.

Evernote: A Success Manual for College Students will guide you through the use of Evernote in nine informative chapters. Each chapter will open you to power new ideas to bring more organization into your college experience with less stress.

Chapter One will introduce you to Evernote, provide you with reasons why you should use this wonderful tool, and highlight the benefits you will receive using it.

Chapter Two will show you how to load Evernote on all your devices to include computers, tablets, and smartphones. I will also take you through an orientation and point out preferences that you should set.

Chapter Three introduces you to the basics of creating notebooks, notes, and tags. You will pick up ideas of documents that you should capture to Evernote prior to beginning college.

Chapter Four focuses on building dynamic checklists to help you stay on task. You will learn about using checklists both in and out of class.

Chapter Five will share strategies for taking notes to support your learning. You will take a deeper look at capturing and organizing notes using different methods.

Chapter Six looks at creating routines to increase efficiency. You will also learn how to set reminders on your notes.

Chapter Seven focuses on retrieving content from Evernote through its powerful search function. You will learn to develop and save search queries to get the exact set of notes you need.

Chapter Eight outlines strategies for using Evernote to complete complex research assignments. Included are techniques for automating your research and using tools like the Web Clipper.

Chapter Nine is all about using Evernote outside of the classroom as you prepare for the next chapter of your life.

I am confident that as you read *Evernote: A Success Manual for College Students,* you will think of many more ways to put Evernote to use. If you get a chance, please share them with me.

Let's get started by learning more about Evernote.

Chapter One

Welcome to Evernote

It finally arrived. Your heart is racing a little bit with anticipation as you look down at that unopened letter. All that work you did has finally paid off. You are going to college. Congratulations!

I know what you are feeling. Being admitted to college is a huge life event, and I want to help you succeed in this new chapter in your book of life. I want to share a fantastic program with you that will help elevate your educational game to the next level. I am going to show in this chapter why you should be using Evernote for everything you do.

Once Upon a Time ...

When I started college, there were no computers, iPads, or cell phones. You did everything with paper and pencil. Teachers gave you stacks and stacks of papers for every class. They expected you to have a binder for every class to keep your documents. I was not that organized. My binders were a mess. The covers were falling off and papers were falling out. I lost an untold amount of documents due to an improper filing system. My classmates and I would fill up garbage cans with what I considered trash at the end of a term. I was an organized mess.

We would go through the process all over again each term. Now, professors are still handing out documents but they are digital. The same challenge exists. How do you organize all these documents, create meaningful notes, and use them when you need them? What if there is a better way? There is. Many years later I discovered how. The personal computer was everywhere by the time I was in graduate school, and so were smartphones. More importantly, a new program became available—Evernote.

Why Use Evernote?

You have many academic responsibilities as a student. You must attend classes, do homework, and take part in extracurricular activities. You collect papers, write reports, and track various things to do. You carry around many notebooks, scraps of paper, and thoughts. Have you ever lost a critical document? Have you ever wasted time trying to find a report you "knew" you had?

I had a separate notebook for each high school class. There were piles and piles of class handouts, which I stuffed in my textbooks. Not to mention the documents from the extracurricular programs in which I was a member. I shoved many of these papers into the bottom of my gym bag. The documents would come out in much worse shape than when they went in. I wasted a lot of time and disrupted my learning in high school because I lacked organization.

Staying organized is one of the keys to your success. It is what I will be focusing on. Evernote will help your organizational skills. You can digitize and store everything you collect in Evernote. You can organize and retrieve information when you need it from any of your devices.

What is Evernote?

Evernote is a digital notebook and database. It can capture and store notes, pictures, audio files, documents, ideas, to-do lists, and much more. The program is a cloud-based application available from all your devices. Evernote will sync content to all your devices when you add a note or document. Synchronizing content means you can access all your materials from any device running Evernote. You can and should install Evernote on your computers, phones, and tablets.

Figure 1. An example of an Evernote desktop.

You can share what you create and upload with others such as a notebook or individual notes with your study group members. Group members could also add their notes or make changes to notes if you allow them.

I will go into more detail later about how you can use Evernote, but here are some ideas to get you thinking.

• You can store all the worksheets a teacher gives you. You will never lose a worksheet again.

• You can also upload your finished homework.

• You can take class notes directly into Evernote. You will have one place to go when it comes time to study.

• Why lug around a heavy textbook to explore a chart on page 115? Take a picture of the chart and have it with you on your cell phone anywhere.

• Do you want to know when your next basketball game is? Upload your schedule to Evernote.

With Evernote, you can organize your content with notebooks and tags. The power of Evernote is that you only need to look in one place for your information.

Benefits

Evernote's power comes from its ability to use it in numerous ways.

- Multiple ways to collect information
- Digital notebook
- Flexible
- No lost notes
- Paperless
- Never forget important information
- Notes can include a variety of content
- Annotate images and PDF documents
- Capture content anytime and anywhere
- Works with other devices and applications
- Platform independent
- Save all your research
- Easy to update your notes
- Easy organize
- Easy to retrieve notes
- Powerful search feature
- Search through PDFs and images
- Mobile use
- Share and collaborate with others

Let's examine these benefits in more depth.

Numerous Ways to Collect Information

Here are the different ways to add a note or content into Evernote. I will guide you through each one and provide ideas for using these note types to support your studies.

- Type in a note
- Email a message to Evernote

- Scan documents to Evernote

- Clip webpages with the Web Clipper

- Drag documents from your computer into Evernote

- Print a document as a PDF to Evernote

- Capture audio files

- Copy and paste information into Evernote

- Set up automation to capture information as it happens

- Tweet to Evernote

- Handwrite your notes to Evernote

- Capture images

You will want to set up a system where you develop the habit of capturing everything. You should strive for a paperless system. Imagine if you didn't have to drag all those books and papers around your school! Evernote makes that dream a reality.

Digital Notebook

Evernote is a digital notebook, a place where you can add and organize everything. You can store assignments, schedules, syllabi, class notes, pictures of whiteboards, homework, locker combination, workout tips, etc.

You can organize everything in its own notebook. You can store your chemistry notes separately from your basketball drills. You can then retrieve a note when you need it most.

This digital notebook will handle all kinds of note types. Your notes can be text files, images, PDF documents, other file types, handwritten notes, webpages, audio files, and more.

You can create notes with a size of 25Mb for free accounts and 200Mb for personal accounts. Additionally, free users can upload 60Mb per month whereas personal account users can upload 10Gb.

You can get a feel for Evernote with a free account. Normal files are only a couple hundred kilobytes per note. This would allow you to create roughly 300 notes each month. I started using Evernote in 2007 and I have created over 8,100 notes. Very few of my files are larger than 25Mb.

Flexible

Flexibility is one of Evernote's most powerful features. You can input various types of content. You can take text-only notes, or you can enhance the notes with documents, images, audio files, and more. You can easily save web pages and then improve them with your notes. You can upload scanned documents or drag and drop documents from your computers.

You can access your notes from any of your devices including desktop, laptop, phone, and tablet. You can get your vital information whenever and from wherever you are.

Organize your notes in untold ways using notebooks and tags. You may want to put all your notes into unique notebooks, or you may want to add a list of tags to your notes. It could even be a combination of both. The great thing is that it is up to you.

Evernote allows you to not only search through all text documents, but you will also search through the images and attached documents.

You can share your notes or keep them to yourself. It is up to you.

You can also bring Evernote to the next level by creating shortcuts to your favorite notebooks, tags, and even search queries. You will be able to increase the speed at which you can get to the information you need.

Evernote will surprise you with the different ways you can use it.

No Lost Notes

These digital notebooks are safe from disaster. You will never lose an important document again. It is a great place to store essential papers. Evernote would be a safe place to keep a copy of all your travel documents and contact lists if you take part as a foreign exchange student. I send all my travel plans and documents to Evernote to include flight information, car rental agreements, and hotel reservations. I pull out my phone rather than sift through a bunch of papers.

You do not lose anything if your phone or computer breaks, because all your information is in the cloud. You log onto another device connected to the internet, and you are back in business.

Many people I know email themselves articles so they can read them later. Email is a poor organizer for important documents or even for things like articles that you want to read at another time. You can instead forward a document or save an article directly to Evernote to view later.

Paperless

One of the features I like is that Evernote is paperless. I filled numerous notebooks with important course notes over my academic career. I also collected thousands of handouts. I have also moved many times. It was a burden to lug all these papers around. The documents took up space and were hard to find when I needed them. Scanning all my documents to Evernote was one of the best decisions I made. I was able to get rid of five stand-up filing cabinets full of materials. Since then, I have never lost a paper, and I can easily share them with other people.

Here are reasons to go paperless: end clutter, save money on storage containers, save time finding things, become more efficient, have a secure backup, and access your documents anytime and anywhere. [1]

Going paperless is not hard. Start by replacing your current note-taking system with Evernote. You can begin by taking pictures of your written notes or scanning them as PDF documents. You can take photos of the whiteboards while you are in class. Finally, you can start typing in your notes. You may have to first clear it with your professor. You will find Evernote hard to live without the more you use it.

Never Forget Important Information

Have you ever showed up someplace only to realize you left an important document sitting back in your room? You will always have access to the necessary papers if you scan your content into Evernote.

Have you ever loaded a piece of software and later needed the access code? Evernote is an excellent tool for storing access codes. It can also store combinations for locks and lockers, computer passwords (encrypt them), instruction manuals, and more.

Evernote's slogan is "Remember everything."

Collect Ideas

Ideas occur anytime and anywhere. I have great ideas when I am out walking, in the gym, or driving through town. I do not usually have a pen and piece of paper handy, but I have my phone. I can type a note to myself in Evernote or use the audio file feature to record and capture my idea. When I get back to my computer, my idea is sitting there ready for me.

You can create a swipe file of ideas with Evernote. A swipe file is traditionally a collection of sales copy and advertising examples. I would like to expand this definition to include any ideas worth saving. Evernote is a useful tool for collecting great ideas, no matter where you find them. You can use a swipe file to collect art ideas, writing ideas, project ideas, and much more. The great thing about Evernote is you can find your ideas later with a quick search. "If you are a creative design student in art, architecture, etc., you can use Evernote to compile ideas around a topic." [2]

The great thing about Evernote is that you can capture an idea wherever you are. Just open up your phone, tablet, or computer. You don't even need an internet connection when you capture the idea. Evernote will sync to the cloud once you connect back to the internet.

Notes Can Include a Variety of Content

You can capture everything to Evernote. The real power is combining different media. You can start a note with an audio recording then add text for more clarification. Imagine being in a class. You could record the class lecture, add your text notes, throw in some images of the whiteboard, and include the class handouts all in one note.

Annotate Images and PDF Documents

Wouldn't it be great if you could mark up the documents and images you store in Evernote? The great news is you can. You can enhance content with annotations once you load images or PDF documents to Evernote.

Capture Content Anytime and Anywhere

Your work or study does not stop because you are offline. You can capture notes regardless of whether you are online or not using Evernote.

You can be hiking without internet access and spend the day collecting notes. Then sync to the cloud for full access once you reconnect to the internet. You can access your information with searches regardless of where you are.

Ensure you sync with the cloud if you wish to access your recent set of notes before you go offline.

Works With Other Devices and Applications

Evernote does not work in isolation. Many programs provide you with the ability to save your final work to Evernote. You can use a program like Penultimate to write on your iPad and then save it to Evernote if you'd rather handwrite than type. Are you an artist? You can use many different drawing programs to capture your sketches to Evernote.

Platform Independent

Evernote is platform-independent. What does this mean? It means Evernote works with the same notes regardless of the device. You can access Evernote on a Windows machine or Mac computer. You can load Evernote on Android and Apple phones as well as on tablets and iPads. I have Evernote loaded on my home computer, work computer, Chromebook, iPad, and Android phone. Evernote is with me wherever I go. You can even access Evernote through your web browser by going to https://Evernote.com.

It also does not matter what device you are on. You can start adding a note on your phone and later finish the document on your computer.

Evernote stores your content on a secure server. This cloud server ensures Evernote shares notes to all your devices. You can retrieve content from anywhere in the world as long as you have an internet connection. Evernote also keeps a copy of your notes on your local devices.

Save All Your Research

Evernote is a fantastic tool for collecting and organizing research materials. I used Evernote to collect ideas and articles to help write this book. You can capture a note as you are thinking about your research. You can use Evernote's Web Clipper to clip entire articles while browsing the web. Evernote saves the whole piece along with a link back to the article. Each note will have a time and date stamp so you know when you clipped the article. A time and date stamp can be important for some research. You can build a citation for your reference using sites like refme.com, Zotero, and Endnote and save it to Evernote.

You are also able to capture different document types, such as presentations and spreadsheets. It is a great place to build out a lab notebook.

You can then use tags and notebooks to help organize all your captured notes. Tags will help you categorize similar ideas.

One of the most significant benefits of collecting your research with Evernote is you can use Evernote for your research throughout your lifetime. You can research a topic throughout school and beyond.

Easy to Update Your Notes

Not only can you add notes to Evernote, but you can also make easy updates. Your best thinking sometimes happens away from the classroom or your study area. You want to capture your ideas when inspiration strikes. Pull out your device to add information to a current note if you have already been working on a problem. You can do this anywhere.

Easy to Organize

Evernote places new notes in a default notebook. Inbox is my default notebook. I can then move notes to other notebooks and add tags to the notes during my note review. Batch organizing is also possible. You can select multiple notes to add tags and change the notebook.

One of the great things about Evernote is you get to choose how you want to organize your content. I will offer suggestions throughout this book, but you create an organization scheme that works for you. Evernote makes it easy for you to change organizations to suit your needs.

Easy to Retrieve Notes

Not only should you develop the habit of capturing information to Evernote in your daily routines, but also to retrieve content from Evernote. Finding information is quite easy. You can conduct a search, review the contents in a notebook, or explore a tag.

Powerful Search Features

Evernote's search function is one of the features I use on a daily basis. Evernote not only searches through titles, but it also searches through the note, attached documents, PDFs, and images. Additionally, you can search based on one or more tags. You can see what items you still need to complete if you create to-do lists with checkboxes. Searching is a powerful way to discover documents in your collection and identify new relationships.[3] Evernote will highlight each use of your search phrase. You can link articles together as you identify connections.

Search Through PDFs and Images

The ability to search through images to find text phrases is one of my favorite features of Evernote. Searching through images means I can take a picture of a sign, business card, whiteboard, etc. Evernote is able to identify text with that search phrase.

Evernote does this with a technology called optical character recognition (OCR). OCR is the conversion of images of typed, handwritten, or printed text into text that machines and we can understand.

One way I use this is by taking pictures of my bookshelves. I have a lot of books. It is sometimes hard to locate a book I know I have. Now I search for the title of the book, and Evernote will show me the picture of the appropriate bookshelf. You need to return the book to the same shelf, or you will have to keep taking new pictures.

Mobile Use

Evernote's mobile application works fantastic. It is easy to pull my phone out of my pocket to capture a note, picture, reminder, or audio file. I have an Evernote widget on the first page of my phone so I can capture notes as well as search for information. It could not be easier.

Do you have a smartphone? Ensure you add Evernote. You will then have all your school materials at your fingertips wherever you go.

Researchers use many different tools, but note-taking, audio recordings, and picture taking are their primary means for capturing relevant information. You can conduct research wherever you are using your smartphone.[4] You can "scan" documents to searchable PDF documents using the document camera mode.

Collaboration/Sharing

Evernote has a powerful sharing capability. You can share a single note or an entire notebook. The note will show the most current version each time it updates. You can also share your notes on Facebook, Twitter, and LinkedIn. Additionally, you can create a link to a note that is available publicly. You can subscribe to notebooks others are sharing with you.

Subscribing to notebooks will let you see the notes inside the notebook and any new notes added.

Why would you want to share your notes? Your instructor may wish to share a notebook of resources with you. In turn, you could create a notebook to share content with your instructor or with your study group. Anyone in the group can add to the notebook. Others can update the notes if the notebook owner shares the notebook with editing permissions. Sharing a notebook with your instructor means your teacher could provide feedback on your work.

You could share the link through email or add it as a link on a website or learning management system if you create a public link to a note.

Some of the benefits of a shared notebook include:

- Saving printing costs

- Notes are always current

- Capture a variety of content

- Easy to share notes and notebooks. [5]

Wrap Up

These benefits are only a glimpse of the power of Evernote. You will begin to understand its full potential when you start using it. I will guide you through installing Evernote and teach you how to use Evernote using scenarios encountered while a student. Additionally, I will share strategies to help you succeed as a student. Let's start by getting ready to go to college.

***

1. Ward, David. Evernote for Lawyers: A Guide to Getting Organized & Increasing Productivity. The Attorney Marketing Center, n.d.

2. "Evernote: A Guide for Academics," The Brain that Wouldn't Die, accessed October 13, 2017, https://brainthatwouldntdie.wordpress.com/2013/09/30/evernote-a-guide-for-academics/.

3. Elisabeth. "How Academics Use Evernote to Make Life Easier." Personal Knowledge Management for Academia & Librarians, July 30, 2013. http://www.academicpkm.org/2013/07/30/how-exactly-do-people-use-evernote-in-academia/

4. ClydeBank Technology. Evernote: Mastery - Exactly How To Use Evernote To Organize Your Life, Manage Your Day & Get Things Done (Evernote, Evernote Essentials, Evernote Mastery, Evernote For Dummies, Time Management). ClydeBank Media LLC, 2014. http://www.amazon.com/dp/B00MLQ4MT6/ref=r_soa_w_d

5. Philip Copeland, "Evernote for Every Choir, Composer, Classroom, and Conductor," Choral Journal 56, no. 1 (August 1, 2015): 49–54.

Chapter Two

Preparing Evernote for College

Can't wait for college to start? I bet you are excited to begin this new stage in your life. Having spent a considerable amount of my life in a college classroom, I can assure you it will be different from high school. Your instructors will tell you about your assignments, but you may or may not receive reminders for when to turn them in. Your professors will hold you to a higher level of responsibility for your learning. The pace of college work is also much faster. You need to track a lot of things. Evernote comes in handy for monitoring your assignments and helping you stay on course. Naturally, you will have your calendar and learning management system to aid you through your academic pursuits but Evernote will provide you with 360-degree support. Evernote is your digital memory and assistant.

There are many things you need to track as you prepare to go to college —even before you step into the classroom. You have to plan your move, get your books, gather essential records, write down emergency contacts, and much more. Evernote will help you with all these tasks.

Let's get started.

Setting Up Evernote for Success

Take a moment to get Evernote installed and set up. You will want to set up a capture kit. A capture kit means installing Evernote on all your computers and mobile devices as well as adding the Web Clipper to all your web browsers. You will then be able to capture notes anytime and anywhere.

In this chapter, you are going to learn how to set up your Evernote preferences for success. Please keep in mind this information is current as I write this chapter. Evernote, like most software companies, continues to update its programs. You may have to look up current procedures if things have changed, but the concepts should remain the same.

I am going to focus on the desktop application for organizing information but point out the power of mobile for collecting and consuming content.

Setting Up an Evernote Account

Begin by going to https://Evernote.com/ and clicking on the "Sign up" link. You should see a page with subscription options. The free version is great for getting started but it restricts you to two platforms. I would recommend using the web or desktop version and one for your mobile device. Select one of the options. Evernote will provide an option to use your Google account if you have one. Otherwise, enter an email address as your username and a strong password. You will see the web version of Evernote once you have clicked on the continue button. Evernote will also encourage you to create your first note.

Installing Evernote on Your Devices

Now that you have an account it is time to load Evernote on all your computers and mobile devices. Be selective if you are using a free account otherwise go nuts and put Evernote everywhere. You are also going to install the Web Clipper on all your web browsers. The Web Clipper will prove an essential tool for your school research. It allows you to capture web pages directly to Evernote where you can mark them up or add your own notes. I will tell you a lot more about Web Clipper in Chapter Eight.

Load Evernote everywhere because it is hard to use Evernote if you do not have access to it. You want to make it as easy as possible to capture, organize, share, and retrieve your notes. You gain the most benefit when you develop a habit of using Evernote. One key to developing a habit is to set up your environment to succeed. [1]

Evernote updates the web version weekly. There is nothing you will need to do to keep it current.

Installing Evernote on Your Computers

Go to https://Evernote.com/download to install Evernote for your computer. Evernote has installers for Windows PC and Macs. The program should start to download. There is a download link if the application does not begin to download.

Run the installer for your computer type. Accept the license agreement as the program loads. I use the recommended installation and do not make any changes. Sign in once the program loads. You should be ready to use Evernote. The web version of Evernote and the desktop application look very similar.

Evernote Orientation and Setting Preferences

Let's take a guided tour of Evernote then I will show you how to load Evernote on your mobile devices. Knowing where to find your main tools is important. We will begin with the desktop and web versions of Evernote. There may be slight differences between computer types. I am using a Windows PC.

I'll provide some suggestions for setting your preferences. You will have to play with Evernote to discover which setup works best for you.

Desktop and Web Orientation

Evernote Desktop has four major components: toolbar, sidebar, notes list, and note view. You will spend most of your time in the notes list and note view. Let's see what is available in each. But, before we do that, let's look at the Home page.

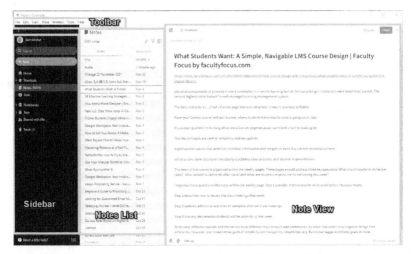

Figure 2. Evernote Desktop showing the toolbar, sidebar, notes list, and note view.

Home

You will see the **Home** page when you first start Evernote. The **Home** page will provide you with easy access to recent and suggested notes. You will have access to a scratchpad for jotting down quick ideas. There is an area for pinned notes as well as recently captured web clips, images, documents, audio files, and emails. Additionally, there are widgets for your notebooks, tags, and shortcuts. We will talk about these different elements throughout the book.

The **Customize Home** button will provide you with the ability to set up your home page to work for you. You can add and remove widgets. Additionally, you can move widgets around as well as resize them. It is important to note that customizing the home page is a personal account feature.

Toolbar

The toolbar is at the top of the program. It has seven major menu items. You can activate many of the tools with a keyboard shortcut combination. You will want to learn these time-saving keyboard shortcuts as you become more comfortable with Evernote.

Note: Some of the features are only available with a Personal subscription. Yet, there is quite a bit you can do with the free version of Evernote.

Click on each of the menu items as I discuss them.

File. The **File** menu item allows you to create new things such as notes, notebooks, and tags. You are also able to import and export items with Evernote. At some point, you may want to export all your Evernote notes as a backup. Finally, you will be able to log out of Evernote (it will continue to run in the background) as well as quit Evernote, which stops it completely.

Edit. The **Edit** menu provides tools to help you manipulate text. You will be able to cut, copy, and paste text as well as undo mistakes you may have made. You can either select all your notes or select everything within a note with the **Select All** feature. Finally, you can activate the Evernote search function. The **Switch to** option allows you to jump to a specific notebook, tag, or note. Start typing in a topic of interest and the list will filter based on your query. Select an item from the displayed list.

View. The first two controls allow you to move back and forward through your usage history like the back button on a web browser. Evernote lets you change how much you can see with the actual size, zoom in, zoom out, and toggle full-screen options. You can display or hide the left-hand menu. The **hide/show** sidebar will switch between icon-only navigation to one that also has textual prompts. There is an option to toggle the note count for navigation items on and off. The **Dark Mode** setting will let you switch between a dark screen and a light one.

Note. The **Note** menu provides several tools that help you best use a note. For example, you may prefer to work on a note in a separate window. You can also share your notes with another person.

You can also copy and move notes to other notebooks from the **Note** menu. Additionally, you can add tags to one or many notes. You can throw a note into the trash can if no longer needed. The **Note** menu is where you go if you want to merge notes into one note. You must first select more than one note. Other options under the **Note** menu include duplicating a note, conducting a find and replace within a note, printing a note, and editing tags. Finally, you can see the history of the note as well as get some stats on the note.

Window. The **Window** menu has two options: close the Evernote window or minimize the window. Evernote is a mouse click away when you close it. You can find it in the Windows taskbar notification area. You will first have to expand the notification area to see running applications. An Evernote button will remain on the taskbar if you just minimize Evernote.

Tools. The next menu item is **Tools**. The first option under the **Tools** menu is a link to your account info. The account info page will let you see and change:

- Personal settings
- Devices to which you are connected
- Profile information
- Reminder settings
- Context sources for searches
- Security summary
- Applications that have access to your account
- Access history
- Connected services
- Account status (you can deactivate or close your account)
- Purchase history if you are on a personal or business account

The **Tools** menu will also let you toggle the settings for spell checking while you are typing and saving data when you log out.

Help. The last menu item is **Help**. You can find links to Evernote's Help and Learning webpages. You can send Evernote your questions as well as find tutorials on how to use different functions from these pages. I have explored these pages in-depth as I got to know Evernote. They even have tips for students.

A **Quick Tour** provides a brief orientation to the Evernote layout. You can find a list of keyboard shortcuts. This page will let you change the keyboard shortcut as well as disable it. Finally, you can check for upgrades, find release notes, and check your activity logs. The logs can be useful if you are troubleshooting an issue. Speaking of troubleshooting, Evernote provides a small toolset to help you resolve a problem.

Sidebar

You will access many of the resources you need via the sidebar found on the left side of the screen. Starting from the top, you can find links that allow you to create new notes, access your shortcuts, see all your notes, access your notebooks, check on shared content, view your tags, and see what's in the trash.

You can control if you wish to display the sidebar or not, as well as what items you want to be listed. You can access extra menu features such as creating a notebook or tag by right-clicking on the different menu items.

Let me touch on each sidebar item. I will share more on many of these items as we proceed.

Account. The first option focuses on your account. Evernote does allow you to have more than one account. You could add each account through this menu option and switch between them. Selecting the account info menu item will take you to your account. I described account information in the Tools menu section.

Search. You can start a search by typing in the search field. You will see your search narrow with every keystroke. Clicking on the search field will show you recent searches, saved searches, and search filters. I have shared an entire section on conducting searches in Chapter Seven. Searching is a powerful strategy for recovering your notes.

New Note. You can start a new blank note when you click on the **New Note** link. Clicking on the **New Note** link is only one way to add a note but a common one. Clicking on the associated drop-down arrow will present a list of templates that you can use to start your note. There are templates for meeting notes, to-do lists, lecture notes, essay outlines, meal planners, and daily reflections. You can choose from many other templates when you start a blank note. You can also craft and save your notes as reusable templates.

Home. Clicking on the **Home** menu item will take you to the home screen that I described above.

Shortcuts. **Shortcuts** is where you can access your favorite notes, notebooks, tags, and search queries. You can drag a high-use notebook or note to the shortcuts area for quick access. You can add advanced search queries to your shortcuts if you use them often. For example, I have a query that searches for any to-do items I have not checked. Clicking on the **Shortcuts** title will expand and collapse that menu part.

Notes. The **Notes** link lets you see a list of all your notes. The **Notes** link is quite useful for quick access to all your notes.

Notebooks. The **Notebooks** link allows access to the different notebooks you created. You will see a list of all your notes in the selected notebook. It is also possible to stack notebooks to help with organization. I will provide more details on notebooks and stacks in Chapter Three.

Tags. The **Tags** menu item gives you quick access to all your tags. A tag is a word to help categorize your note. For example, you could tag all the notes you take during biology class with a biology tag. You could use an appropriate tag to mark all your jazz band notes, making them easier to locate. You can create up to 100,000 tags. I use a lot of tags.

Shared With Me. You will find a list of notes or notebooks shared with you. You will receive an invitation to accept a notebook before it will appear.

Trash. Finally, you can see all the notes you have placed in the trash, at least until you empty the trash. You must empty the trash to permanently delete notes.

Upgrade. You will see an upgrade link if you are still on a free account. As much as I like Evernote, I recommend that you test Evernote before upgrading.

Notes List

The **Notes List** is available when you select a sidebar menu item such as a search query shortcut, a specific notebook, or a tag. Choosing one of these items will filter your view to show a list of appropriate notes. The notes list will display just to the right of the sidebar.

You will see how many notes you have, a sort button, a filter button, a tag search button. Selecting a notebook or saved search will provide you with a more options button. The menu items under more options will vary depending upon your starting point. You will be able to add new notes; share, rename, or delete a notebook; set the notebook as a default notebook, move a notebook to a stack; add the notebook to stack; or export a notebook if you start by clicking on a notebook. Starting from a saved search will enable you to edit or delete the search query.

You will see your note displayed in the note view panel when you select a note from the notes list. You can select more than one note if you want to change the notebook or tag for the selected notes. Selecting more than one note will enable you to merge them together. You can choose a group of notes at one time using the **Shift** key. Just click on the first note and then the last note of the series. You use the **Ctrl** key and click on notes, not in a series.

Setting Notes List Preferences

The first place to start setting preferences is by setting up your views. There is a view options tool at the top of the **Notes List** that will let you decide how to display your notes:

- Card View
- Snippet View
- Side List View
- Top List View

You can also decide which columns that you want to include on the list. You can choose from the following:

- Date updated
- Date created
- Location
- Tags
- Reminder date
- Created by
- Updated by
- Size
- URL

You sort your notes using the title, date created, or date updated column headings. I recommend that you add only the columns that you need. You will not be able to see all the columns unless you scroll side to side. The columns are available when using the side list and top list views.

Note View

Finally, we get to the **Note View**. The note view is where you see your note.

The note title and other tools are at the top of the note. You can change the title if you wish. There are strategies for creating a title that will help you find the note. I will share these strategies later when we look at creating notes in Chapter Three. You will see its notebook and last edited date above the title. There is a share button in the upper right corner. Next is a drop-down menu with many more options. Some of the capabilities include moving or copying the note, adding it to the shortcuts menu, exporting the note, and printing it.

Change the notebook by mousing over the current notebook and selecting the button that pops up. You can only place a note in one notebook at a time.

You add tags and reminders to a note at the bottom of the note view. You can add up to 100,000 tags per note, but you shouldn't.

Clicking within the note will bring up an edit menu so you can enhance your note. You can find options to change the font, font size, color, and style. There are highlighting tools and a tool to add code to your note. You can create bulleted lists, numbered lists, and to-do lists. You can also align text as well as indent and outdent text. You have the capability of creating tables and adding horizontal lines. You can enhance your note by adding items like Google documents, audio clips, images, tables, horizontal lines, and more.

That is a full tour of the Evernote desktop and web version. Let's take a tour of what you will see on an iPad. The mobile tour will be shorter because many of the tools and features will be the same.

Install Evernote on Your Mobile Devices

Load Evernote on all your mobile devices to get the most benefit. Go to the Apple Store if using an Apple iPad or iPhone. Likewise, you will need to go to the Google Play Store if you have an Android device. Just search for Evernote.

You will need to log in with your Evernote account information once you download and install the app.

Taking a Look at the Mobile Experience on the iPad

I am going to focus on the iPad experience rather than address each mobile type since each mobile application has a similar performance. Nonetheless, it is best to review Evernote's tutorials because Evernote updates different applications often. It would be impossible to keep up with the changes.

Let's look at the iPad. I prefer to view it in the landscape mode when I use Evernote on an iPad. This view makes it easier for me to see the note. Evernote on the iPad has many of the features of the desktop, but not all. It also has a couple of features not found on the desktop and web versions. Getting to know what is available is essential.

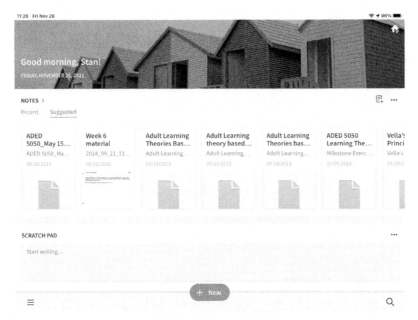

Figure 3. Evernote on the iPad

The initial view of the Evernote iPad app consists of a stack of widgets that you can customize. You will see a welcome screen at the top of the application with a Home customization button. Selecting the button will show you the list of widgets. The red circle with a line in it will allow you to delete that widget. You can also rearrange the order of the widgets.

There are three options at the bottom of the screen: navigation menu, New note menu, and the search function. I will describe these in more depth in a few minutes.

Home Screen

The home screen of the Evernote iPad app consists of a series of widgets. As I noted, you can decide which widgets you want to use as well as the order that you want to have them available if you have a personal account. Let's take a look at the different widgets.

Notes. The Notes widget will display a series of note thumbnails. You have the option of seeing recent notes or suggested notes. Selecting a note will open the note into its own screen. Clicking on the **Notes** title for the widget will display a notes list.

Scratch Pad. The scratch pad is a convenient writing area where you can take quick notes. You can clear the scratch pad or convert what you have written into a note. You can find this capability with the menu in the upper right corner of the widget.

Pinned Note. Do you have a note that you refer to every day? Perhaps it is your to-do list. You can keep your to-do list front and center with the pinned note widget. Select the note that you want to pin. You can conduct a search or scan through your notebooks. You can also view a note and select **Pin to Home** from the menu.

Recently Captured. The **Recently Captured** widget will show you thumbnails of all your rich media notes. You can choose from web clips, images, documents, audio, and emails. Selecting a note will open it for your review.

Notebooks. The **Notebooks** widget will show thumbnails of your recent and suggested notebooks. The thumbnails also display how many notes are in the notebook. As you would expect, selecting a notebook will open the notebook and display a list of notes. Clicking on the **Notebooks** title for the widget will display a notebooks list.

Tags. The **Tags** widget will present your most used tags along with a count of the number of notes with an associated tag. Clicking on a tag will display a list of notes related to the tag. Clicking on the **Tags** title for the widget will display a tags list.

Shortcuts. The **Shortcuts** widget will show you a list of your favorite shortcuts. Clicking on the **Shortcuts** title for the widget will display a list of all your shortcuts.

You may not know how these different tools work but you will soon. I will not only show you how to use each tool but also explain how you can improve your success in college. Let's continue our review of the iPad application.

Navigation Menu

Click on the navigation menu button in the lower-left corner of the application to see the navigation menu. It is three stacked lines. You will be able to access your account, the home screen, shortcuts, notes, notebooks, tags, shared with me files, and trash. Close the navigation menu by either sliding it to left, tapping on another part of the screen, or clicking on the Home menu item.

You will be able to access the following capabilities through the navigation menu.

Account. The **Account** button will display a menu allowing access to your account, subscription details, synced devices, email account, and sign out. You can also switch between accounts if you have more than one account.

Upgrade. You should see a button at the top of the menu to upgrade to the personal version. It will go away once you upgrade. You should first know if you like Evernote before considering to upgrade. I am delighted with Evernote enough to be a subscriber.

Home. Clicking on the **Home** menu item will close the navigation menu and return you to the home screen.

Shortcuts. The **Shortcuts** button will show a list of recent notes and all your shortcuts. Shortcuts can link to specific notes, notebooks, tags, or saved searches.

Notes. Selecting the Notes option will bring you to the Notes page. You will see a list of all your notes on the left-hand side of the screen. The right side of the screen displays a selected note. You have the ability to add new notes. You can filter the notes list using the search function.

This screen also provides you with the ability to edit your note. Selecting the **Edit** button will present you with a robust editing menu. You will be able to insert a wide array of rich media as well as mark up your text like a word processing program.

There are many tools available to you at the top of the note. These tools will allow you to share your note, add tags, add reminders, add to shortcuts, pin the note, print the note, and much more. I encourage you to explore this menu.

Notebooks. Clicking on the **Notebooks** menu item will display a notebooks list. There is a search tool to help you locate a notebook. The notebooks list will list all the notebooks and stacks along with the number of notes in each notebook. Selecting a notebook will open the notebook and display a list of notes. You will also see the note editing window.

Tags. The **Tags** menu option works like the Notebooks menu item. Selecting the **Tags** menu option will display all your tags. Next to each tag is the number of notes associated with that tag. Clicking on a tag will take you to the notes list filtered for the tag.

Shared With Me. Choosing **Shared with Me** will show you a list of notes that others shared with you. You can add these notes by clicking on the **Add** button. Clicking on the note will allow you to edit the note.

Trash. Finally, the **Trash** menu option will display a list of notes that are in your trash. Selecting a note will show you a view-only representation of the note. The menu in the upper right corner of the note will allow you to restore the note. You can also delete the note forever.

New Note and Search

You can find the add new note and search function on the bottom of the home screen.

New Note. By selecting the **New Note** menu (^), you can add reminders, record audio messages, begin sketches, add attachments, take a photo, scan a document, or start a blank note. You can start with a blank note or begin with a template. A template is a pre-formatted note. Templates will save you time crafting typical notes such as meeting notes, class notes, or even fitness logs. Evernote has hundreds of pre-designed templates to choose from, or you can create your own.

Search. The **Search** button will display a list of your recent searches and saved searches. Saving your useful searches is important. You can also start a new search. You have the option to apply filters when conducting a search by selecting the filter button. You can then select reminders, tags, notebooks, attachments, creation date, and updated date.

Note View

The **Note View** shows you how your note looks. The **Note View** has two primary menu bars: Options and Editing Toolbar.

Options. The **Options** menu sits at the top of the note. There is an option to expand the note to the full screen. You can share your note with others or create a sharable link. You can add tags to the note. There is also an options button. The **Options** button presents a list of functions to include:

- Share Note
- Find in Note
- Add tag
- Add reminder
- Add to Shortcuts
- Pin to Home
- Note info
- Copy internal link
- Print note
- Move note
- Duplicate note
- Save as template
- Delete note

Editing Toolbar. The **Editing Toolbar** will appear when you start to edit your note. Click on a point in your notes where you want to make changes or additions to access the editing toolbar. You can also click on the **Edit** button. The keyboard will appear when you begin to edit a note. Here are the tools you will see from left to right above the keyboard on the Editing Toolbar:

- **Insert**. Selecting the **Insert** option will allow you to choose from the following rich media items:

  1. Camera

  2. Image

  3. Table

  4. Audio

  5. Code Block

  6. Attachment

  7. Link

  8. Divider

  9. Checkbox

  10. Sketch

- **Text formatting**. The **Text Formatting** button will allow you to size your text small, medium, or large. You can choose heading styles. This option also allows you to align your text, change the color of the text, and highlight blocks of text. Strikeout, subscript, and superscript are also available.

- **Text styles**. The next three buttons allow you to bold, italicize, and underline your text.

- **Color**. The next two buttons allow you to color or highlight your text.

- **Lists**. You have the option of creating bulleted, numbered, and checkbox lists.

- **Indent**. Finally, you can indent and outdent blocks of text.

Evernote Widget App for Phone

The Evernote Widget App for my phone is one of the tools I use all the time. It is a small app that allows you to capture different types of notes at a tap of a button. It displays on your phone as a bar with five actions you can take. You can determine which of the functions you want to show. The possible tools include text notes, cameras, audio, reminder, search, simple note, handwriting, and attachment. You can also decide upon the notebook. This app is available for Android and iOS mobile devices.

The widget installs when you install the Evernote app on your phone. Just find a blank place on your phone, hold your finger on the screen until your device allows you to install a widget, then select the Evernote widget from the list.

Select the widget setting button when you want to update it. Just toggle the tools on and off. Note: only five tools show at one time.

Install the Web Clipper

Web Clipper is a powerful browser tool you should install on all your web browsers. You never know which browser you will be using, and you do not want to miss out on capturing an essential article. I use the tool almost daily to clip articles and article segments I find on the internet.

Installing the Web Clipper add-on for your browsers is easy. Regardless of your web browser type, go to https://Evernote.com/features/webclipper. Select the **Get Web Clipper** button. Evernote recognizes the browser you are using and will offer the correct add-on.

You will see the Evernote elephant on your browser's toolbar after installing the add-on. Sign in with your Evernote account the first time you click on the Web Clipper. Evernote will remember your login credentials for 30 days.

You may have to refresh the webpage you want to clip if you immediately try to use the Web Clipper after logging on.

Setting Your Web Clipper Preferences

The Web Clipper will start to learn your behavior and start predicting the notebook in which you will want to place the articles. You can dictate which notebook and tags to use by updating the Web Clipper options. Do this by right-clicking on the Web Clipper tool and select **Options**. You can change the performance of the tool, such as selecting a default notebook location or use smart filing. Other options you can change include tag selection, default clip action, and actions after clipping an article.

You can also access the options menu when you begin to clip an article. You can click on the **Settings** button at the bottom of the Web Clipper dialog box to get to the options.

You should set your default notebook to your Inbox notebook (more in Chapter Three). I would also recommend selecting the **Automatically Close Clipper** option from the **After Clip** section.

Add Your Email Address

We are almost ready to start putting Evernote to work. Evernote provides you with a unique email address to which you can send or forward messages. You should add this email address as a contact in all your email programs such as Outlook and Gmail.

You can find your Evernote email account by selecting **Tools** --> **Account Info** on the desktop program. Evernote will open the accounts information on a web browser. The Evernote email address is in the **Email Note to** section of the Account Summary. Right-click on the address and select copy. Next, open up your email program and follow the procedures for creating a contact. I recommend calling the contact "Evernote."

Getting a Bluetooth Keyboard

You may want to consider purchasing a portable Bluetooth keyboard if you take a lot of notes on your mobile devices.[2] A keyboard will make note-taking so much easier and save you time. My iPad case has a built-in keyboard.

Wrap Up

You are now responsible for organizing your life. Your parents, teachers, and coaches will no longer be managing your calendar, maintaining your to-do lists, or seeing that you are ready for your exams. That is all on you. Your instructors expect you to prepare for their classes.

Tools like Evernote will help you do this with ease. You should now have Evernote loaded on your computers and mobile devices. Load the Web Clipper on all your web browsers. You should also have your Evernote email address added to your contacts list. You are now ready to put Evernote into action. See you in the next chapter.

***

1. Clear, James. Atomic Habits: Tiny Changes, Remarkable Results: An Easy & Proven Way to Build Good Habits & Break Bad Ones. New York: Avery, an imprint of Penguin Random House, 2018.
2. Samuel, Alexandra. Work Smarter with Evernote. Harvard Business School Publishing Corporation, 2013.

Chapter Three

Using Evernote to Prepare for College

Let's put Evernote to use as you prepare to move to college. You have a lot to do. You need to pull together moving lists, get your essential documents loaded, and prepare for your classes. Evernote can help with all this.

In this chapter, you are going to learn about notebooks, notes, and tags. These are the critical elements for your Evernote success. You will load essential documents using these elements that will help you succeed as you get ready to move.

Evernote Basics

Evernote is not only a useful tool for keeping track of everything in your academic and working life but your personal life also. It can serve as a notebook for all those essential documents you need to keep close. These documents can be anything, including receipts, pictures, medical information, family tree information, etc. We are going to focus on documents that will help you with your move. I will share some ideas with you. You take it from there.

I'll show you how to do some of the basics like creating notebooks, notebooks stacks, and creating notes by typing and scanning before I start sharing ways to put Evernote to use. We will then build on these skills.

Notebooks

There are many different ways to organize your notes. Some only use notebooks, others use only tags, yet, many of us use a combination of tags and notebooks. Some Evernote users have created elaborate schemes to organize notes. My use of notebooks and tags has shifted back and forth. There is no right way except that the method has to work for you. Make adjustments to the scheme if it is not working for you.

You will want to organize your notebooks, notebook stacks, and tags so that you keep your top priorities front and center. Let me tell you about notebooks, notebook stacks, and tags. I will also provide you with organizational schemas to consider.

What are Notebooks?

Notebooks are a collection of notes. "As a general rule, notebooks and stacks are useful for collections of information, ideas, or inspiration that you'll want to refer to repeatedly."[1] Notebooks are like folders if you are using a desktop computer. They provide an opportunity to organize notes around a common theme. Evernote will allow up to 250 notebooks. This limit should be adequate for most people.

Figure 4. Example of a notebook with associated notes.

You can further organize notebooks into notebook stacks. For example, you may have created notebooks around your different classes, such as math, English, and history. You could collect these notebooks into a notebook stack called Courses.

You can place notes in one notebook at a time. It is the physical location of the note. Likewise, you can put a notebook into only one notebook stack.

Default Notebook

A default notebook is a special notebook. You have one notebook as your "default" notebook. I recommend that you create a new notebook called "Inbox." Set this notebook as your default notebook.

Everything saves to this notebook unless you choose another notebook for new notes.

Your default notebook should be a temporary holding bin. It is a place where created or added notes will go. You should review this notebook at least weekly. Place the notes into permanent notebooks. I will explain more in Chapter Six as you plan your day.

Creating a Notebook

Creating a new notebook is easy. You will see a "+" plus sign when you mouse over the **Notebooks** tool on the sidebar. Click on the "+" plus sign. Next, give the notebook a name. You could also click on **New Notebook** at the bottom of the notebook list.

Mobile devices operate in a different manner. You will first need to navigate to the notebooks section. Click on the **Add Notebook** tool at the top of the notebook list to create a notebook.

One Notebook Versus Many Notebooks

There are two schools of thought when creating notebooks. One group advocates for creating only one notebook. They rely on tags and searches. This group feels that multiple notebooks can be too complicated. They do not believe creating a hierarchical system is worth the energy. The other school believes in using many notebooks. I am of the multiple notebook clan.

One Notebook

As David Ward remarks in his book, *Evernote for Lawyers: A Guide to Getting Organized & Increasing Productivity*, separate notebooks may slow you down if you rely on the search function to find your notes. One-notebook users are actually two-notebook users. They have an extra notebook to place processed notes besides the inbox notebook. The inbox notebook helps collect all your notes. You would move the note into the processed notebook once you have reviewed the note and updated it with proper tags, titles, and details.

Multiple Notebooks

I am a fan of multiple notebooks and notebook stacks. I prefer to build a logical system in which to place all my notes. For example, I have created a notebook stack called Courses. I have added notebooks for all the courses I have ever taken within that stack. I have placed appropriate course notes into each of the notebooks. Another notebook stack called Organizations holds separate notebooks for different program and group records and meeting notes.

I can still search through all my notes even though my notes are in notebooks. You can do this by first selecting the **Notes** button in the sidebar.

Stacking Notebooks

You can stack or combine your notebooks into a larger notebook called a stack. You can build a stack for all your courses. You can create another stack for all your extracurricular activities or work responsibilities. Group them by semesters if you do want to put all your notebooks into a course stack.

Stacked notebooks can only be one level deep.

You stack notebooks in the sidebar. There are two ways to stack notebooks. The first way is to click on the notebook then while holding the mouse button down, drag the notebook, and drop it on another notebook. The two notebooks create a notebook stack called Notebook Stack. Right-click on the notebook stack title to rename it. Add a notebook to a stack by dragging and placing it on an already established notebook stack.

The other way to create a notebook stack is to right-click on a notebook and select Add to Stack. You will then see a list of current stacks as well as an option for New Stack. Add the notebook to the stack by selecting one of the existing stacks. Evernote will create a new stack called Notebook Stack if you choose the New Stack option. You can then rename the stack.

Temporary Notebooks

Using temporary notebooks is another strategy to consider.[2] You could create a temporary notebook to help manage short-lived events. For example, I created a temporary notebook to help support the writing of this book. I will remove the notebook or archive it when I finish this project. You could create a temporary notebook to track all the details if you are in a club and planning some type of event. I have also used temporary notebooks to help organize all my notes related to a trip.

Brandon Collins, the author of *The 2 Hour Guide to Mastering Evernote - Including: Tips, Uses, and Evernote Essentials*, also has a "General Notes" notebook. He will tag the notes with the details of the event and move them all into the general notes notebook. He will then delete the temporary notebook when finished with it.

Notes

A note is the most basic element of your system. It is one chunk of information that can share meaning on its own. Everything you capture as part of a single meeting would constitute a single note. You should take one note for each class period. You would also include any attachments for the class as well as pictures of the whiteboards or slide presentations in that note. [3]

Naming Your Notes

You will want to name notes in a way that will help you understand what they are about weeks later. I can only scratch my head, wondering what I was thinking at the time when I look at the titles of some of my notes. Here are some strategies to consider when naming notes:

• Start with the date in the yearmoda form then add the rest of your title if the creation date is essential. For example, YYYYMMDD would be 20190220 for 20 February 2019. This format produces clean sorts.

• Be as specific as possible when naming your note. Include these items as appropriate:

1. Main topic

2. Person

3. Location

4. Other important information

Another strategy to consider is numbering notes. Numbering notes within a notebook will help control the order of the notes. "You can control the order by adding numbers to the beginning of the title of the note. For example, "001 - Table of Contents", "01 - Chapter 1", etc."[4]

You will start to see connections between notes in relation to note names. Additionally, Evernote will not only search through notes but also will search through the titles. Being able to search through the title is why deciding on a naming structure is important.

Setting aside time to name every note you capture is important. Make this at least a weekly function, if not daily. Letting notes stack up without proper names will cause frustration later. I speak from experience.

Capturing Different Types of Notes

Evernote provides many ways to create a note from typing in content to dragging in a file. I am going to share different ways to create a note. I encourage you to practice with all the methods.

Typing in a Note

The most basic note is a textual note. You can also use text to enhance other notes. Use text notes to capture ideas, report your findings, or draft a written document.

Click on the **New Note** button and begin typing to start a text note. You can also copy and paste text into the note field to start a note or add new content.

You can enhance your note with styles, highlighting, and color with the Editing toolbar. You can also add other note elements such as images, attachments, and audio files.

Select a notebook and tags for the note once finished drafting it. The title of your note will be the first line of content unless you change it. As I explained earlier, I recommend changing it to something that can help you locate it later.

Add notes to Evernote if you think this information is important to remember later. Here are some ideas of textual notes to get you started:

- Take notes during class.

- Do you belong to a club or work? You can take notes during meetings.

- Draft answers to assignments, blog posts, or other written assignments.

- Capture ideas for projects or new business ventures.

- Collect information on the new contact you met.

- Secure software keys, lock combinations, gaming hacks, etc.

Attaching Documents to Notes

Evernote allows you to collect all kinds of digital documents. These documents can be receipts, homework assignments, class schedules, transcripts, etc. You simply have to add them to Evernote. There are different ways to attach a document in Evernote. You can use the attachment tool, send to Evernote, drag and drop the document into Evernote, or create a notebook that automatically adds documents to Evernote.

Using the Attachment Tool

You can click on the attachment tool if you are editing a note. It looks like a paper clip. This tool will open a file selection dialog box. You can then select a file and click the open button.

Send to Evernote

Right-click on a file and select the **Send to -> Evernote** option if you are in your file manager.

Drag and Drop Documents

You can drag and drop documents into Evernote to either start a note or add a document to an already created note. The process is quite easy. You open up your file manager and select one or more of the files you want to add and drag them to Evernote. You will start a new note if you drag the file(s) to the notes list. Evernote will add the documents to a note if you drag them to an open note.

Automate With an Evernote Folder

Another possibility to add documents is through the use of an automation folder. You can automatically add notes to Evernote when you drop files into a specially designated folder on your computer desktop.

Select **Tools** -> **Import folder...** to set up this notebook. Next, click on the **Add...** button. Select the notebook you wish to use. You can check some options such as if it has subnotebooks, which notebook to place the documents, and if you wish to keep a copy of the document. Click on the **OK** button after making the changes.

Having an automation folder is magical. I set up scripts using programs like IFTTT and Zapier that would gather information and dump it into a special folder I created. The documents would automatically go to Evernote.

Using Attached Documents

I would like to remind you that all documents, including PDF documents, are searchable. You can change the option to either show PDF documents as attachments or embed them within the note.

The ability to annotate a document is another benefit of working with PDFs in Evernote. Just right-click on the PDF and select **Annotate this PDF**. The tools allow you to add arrows, draw boxes, add text, highlight or draw on sections, and apply stamps.

Want to add clarity to your textbook? You can scan and add PDFs of different sections of your book. You can then annotate the PDFs to add clarity. Do you have to comment on an image, website, or another visual object? Capture it as a PDF and annotate it. You can then export the PDF and submit it as part of your assignment. You can also annotate images.

Scanning Documents

Scanning documents is one of the most efficient ways to add documents to Evernote. Evernote will be able to search through the scanned file because it will often be a PDF file. Choose a scanner that will send notes to Evernote. Many offer this feature. I use a ScanSnap 1500. It will scan a stack of documents in seconds. I recommend a flatbed scanner if you are scanning images or books. However, there are scanning apps you can install on your phone or other mobile devices.

Evernote will save your scanned document as an attachment in a note. You can then type in more content, add images, and include audio notes. You can organize your note with the rest of your notes. Ensure you rename the files, add your notes, add tags, and assign an appropriate notebook. I will discard the original document when I finish scanning it. I do this only after I verify they are, in fact, in Evernote.

Scanners are a quick way to add essential documents to Evernote. I recommend scanning anything and everything associated with your classes. Consider scanning syllabi, assignments, handouts, quizzes, etc.

Capturing Audio Notes

The audio note tool is one of the Evernote features I use all the time. I capture ideas I have while walking or driving as an audio note. I will listen to the audio note and add typed comments to make it easier to find when I am back at my computer.

A couple of factors controls the length of the note you can capture. The size of the note you can create controls the length of your audio note. It is 25Mb for free users and 200Mb for personal users. It also depends upon your device and how much space is available at the time.

Here are the general steps for creating and saving an audio recording. The instructions vary by device type. Check the instructions on Evernote specific to your device.

- Begin by creating a new note or opening an existing note.

- Click the microphone button from the formatting bar.

- Click **Record** to start recording. A red dot will appear on the Evernote menu bar icon to indicate that a note is currently recording.

- When finished, click **Save** to stop recording and save the audio to your note.

You can save some steps if you select an audio note when you first create the note. Additionally, you can type and record at the same time. It is important to note that the recording will stop and save if you leave that note.

Saving Audio Files as Notes

Do you have some audio files already saved to your computer and wish to save them to Evernote? Just drag the audio files onto a new note in Evernote.

Did you find an MP3 file on a website you want to save? You must first save the file to your computer or mobile device and then save it to Evernote.

Strategies for Using Audio Notes

There are many reasons you would want to capture an audio note. As I mentioned, I capture audio notes when it is not convenient to write the note, such as when I am walking or driving. Here are more ideas for using audio notes:

• Perhaps you want to capture a lecture from your instructor because of complex concepts or your instructor speaks too fast. Ensure you ask for permission first.

• You may need accommodations, and capturing a recording will help you learn better.

• Audio recordings are a great way to collect interviews for research.

• Record yourself giving a presentation or speech. Use the results to improve your presentation.

• Record the steps of a complex task and play them back as you are working through it.

Creating a Note With Email

In the previous chapter, I encouraged you to add your Evernote email address as a contact in your email program. Forward an email to Evernote whenever you get a message that you wish to save. You can forward messages from your desktop or laptop programs, iPad and tablets, and smartphones.

A forwarded email message will go to your default notebook. The default notebook should be your inbox notebook. However, you can send the message to another notebook with some unique additions to your subject line. I will tell you about this shortly.

Evernote will also save the attachments associated with the email message.

Using email to send a message to your Evernote account is simple. Just forward the email to your exclusive email account. Later, you would go into Evernote to organize the message.

Adding It to Notebooks

You can send a message to a specific notebook by adding the @ symbol followed by the name of your designated notebook to the end of your subject line for your message. For this to work, your notebook must already exist in Evernote. Here is an example:

> The format is:
> Email Subject: [Title of note] @[notebook]
> Here is an example:
> My subject line @Processed

Adding Tags

Additionally, you can add tags to your message that Evernote will automatically apply. Add a # sign followed by the name of one of your tags. You could add multiple tags, but you would have to precede each tag with a # sign. Your tags must already exist in Evernote. And they cannot already have a #sign attached to them. Here is an example:

> The format is:
> Email Subject: [Title of note] #[tag]
> Here is my example:
> My subject line #biology #frogs

You could both add tags to it and place it in a notebook with one message. Here is an example:

> The format is:
> Email Subject: [Title of note] @[notebook] #[tag] #[tag]
> Here is my example:
> My subject line @Processed #biology #frogs

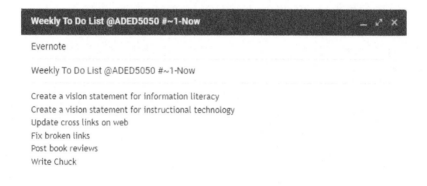

Figure 5. An example of an email message with notebook and tag designations.

Adding Reminders

You can also set reminders related to messages you send to Evernote. Learn more about reminders in Chapter Six. Reminders are a great way to let you know when different assignments are due. You can set a reminder for any note you create. You will use the ! sign. Add a date using this format !yyyy/mm/dd. Here is an example.

The format is:

Email Subject: [Title of note] ![optional date for reminder] @[notebook] #[tag]

My subject line !tomorrow @Processed #biology #frogs

My subject line !2021/09/21 @Processed #biology #frogs

Things to Keep in Mind About Emailing to Evernote

Ensure you follow these guidelines when emailing to Evernote and using the notebook and tag attributes:

- The notebooks and tags must already exist.
- Your notebooks cannot have names with a '@' or a '#' in it.
- Tags cannot have a '#' in the name.
- When writing the subject line follow this order:
- Note title
- Reminder
- Notebook
- Tags

Usually, you can send messages to Evernote by forwarding them. You can also add the Evernote address as a CC or BCC recipient for your message. For example, you might want to reply to a message as well as send a copy to Evernote. In this case, add your Evernote email address to the BCC recipient field.

Resetting Your Email Address

Your Evernote email address is an email address like other addresses. Your email address may get in the hands of spammers even though Evernote randomly generates it. You will want to change it if this happens. You can do this by going to your account page. Navigate to your Evernote email address and click on the **Reset** button. Don't forget to update your new Evernote address in all your address books.[5]

Strategies for Using Email

Here are some strategies to consider for using email as a way to create notes in Evernote. I use many of these every day.

• Forward email messages that are related to your different activities. These notes may come from clubs, teachers, coaches, etc.

• Clean up your email by sending unread newsletters automatically to Evernote. Set up rules to automatically forward messages.

• Pursue a zero inbox strategy by forwarding messages to Evernote.

• Set up Google alerts to track a specific subject. Have those alerts automatically sent to Evernote.

• Set up a Google Voice account with notifications sent to Evernote. Call the account and leave a voice message. Google Voice will transcribe the voice message and automatically forward it to your Evernote account.[6]

Encrypting Notes

Some information is more critical or sensitive than other information. There is information you may want to make more secure than others, even in Evernote. You can do this by encrypting it. You can encrypt an entire note or just parts of it.

Highlight the information that you want to encrypt, right-click on it, and select **Encrypt selected text**. You will then need to provide a secure pass phrase. It is important to remember this pass phrase or you will never recover your information.

Tags

Tags are words you add to a note to help organize and find the note later. Tags help you identify notes that belong to the same collection. They help identify relationships between notes across notes and notebooks. Tags are often extra information not found in the note. For example, you might be on the swim team and have a note for a lifting routine. However, there may not be any sign in the note it relates to the swim team. You could tag the note with "Swim team" to help find it later. Selecting the "Swim team" tag would enable you to see all related notes.

Evernote allows you to create up to 100,000 different tags. I am currently using around 660 tags. Each note can have as many tags as you think appropriate. You should start tagging notes from the day you begin to use Evernote. Tagging provides a great deal of flexibility as you set up your organizational system.

You will be able to filter for a specific tag if you search through all your notes.

How to Tag Notes

Notes you add to Evernote first go to your inbox. At this point, you will clean up the title and description. You should then add tags and place the note into its proper notebook. To add a tag:

1. Select a note to add tags.

2. Click the area called "**Add tag...**". It is at the bottom of the note.

3. Begin typing a word for a tag. You should see it in a list if the word exists.

4. Select the word, and Evernote will add it as a tag. Finish typing the word if the word does not already exist. Evernote will add the new word to your note and the tag list.

5. Continue to add tags as appropriate.

Adding Tags to Multiple Notes

Do you have multiple notes that need the same tag? You do not have to add tags to them one at a time. Select multiple notes from the notes list and select the "**Edit tags...**" option from the bar that appears. Begin adding tags as you would for a single note.

Pre-Creating Tags

You do not have to wait to create new tags only when you are adding them to a note. You can build out your note tagging structure ahead of time.

You can create a tagging structure by moving your cursor over the **Tags** title in the sidebar. Next, click on the "+" plus sign. Enter a new tag in the dialog box that appears. Repeat these steps for each of your new tags.

The tags appear in alphabetical order. You can use different symbols such as hashtags, slashes, and colons to control the order and group them by function. Using symbols also makes them easier to locate.

You can also stack tags like notebooks. Just drag one tag and drop it on another. For example, you may create a tag called projects and stack all the project tags under that tag. This grouping will make finding your project tags easier. Each tag must be unique, even if you stack them.

Here are some ideas for creating your tag structure:

Courses

- Course name and number, e.g., ENG101, MAT103, BIO210, etc.

- Subject, e.g., English, math, biology, etc.

- Grade level, e.g., 100, 200, 500, 600, etc.

- The week when material presented, e.g., /week1, /week2, etc.

- Year, e.g., 2020, 2021, etc.

- Media type, e.g., "class notes," "handouts," "tests," and the like. [7]

Research

- Source: journal, books, newspaper, etc.

- Primary and secondary sources

- Topics: General and specific

- Section topics [8]

- Quotes

- People

- Places

Getting Things Done

- When: use "~" and tag, e.g., ~MIT!, ~1-Now, ~41-Later, ~51-Someday, ~61-Waiting, ~99-Done, XX-Never. Note: MIT is the Most Important Thing

- What: use "/" and tag, e.g., /checklist, /committee, /2019, /2018, etc.

- Who: use ":" and tag, e.g., :Skrabut-Stan, :mom

- Where: use "^" and tag, e.g., ^1313MockingbirdLane

- To do tag: for example, /todo

Figure 6. Example of pre-defined tags

Deleting Tags

Do you have a tag you no longer wish to use? Open the note, click on the tag you want to remove, and press the delete button on your keyboard. You can also click on the down arrow to access the tag's menu select **Remove tag**.

Do you want to get rid of the tag entirely? Click on the "Tags" title, right-click on the tag you want to remove, and select the **Delete tag** menu option. Deleting the tag will remove that tag from all your notes.

Tagging Tips

Here are some essential tips to help you get the most out of your tagging:

•   It is better to tag your notes after you collect them so you can think about relationships between notes rather than tagging notes on the fly.

•   Over time, you will begin to see the connections you have created with your knowledge.

•   Tags are essential to your research. Do not skimp on your tags when doing research. Items you collect for one research project may have value for future projects.

•   Tags will allow you to rapidly find notes on a specific topic.

•   Avoid meaningless words as tags. Try to be as accurate as possible. For example, what does the word "great" mean as a tag? The word "great" does not state the context of the note.

•   Consider using a project tag if you work on projects. You will be able to find all the project notes when you archive your notes and move them to a new notebook.

•   You could create a unique tag that allows you to find essential reference notes. You can find your reference note quicker by adding a distinctive character to the front of the tag. [9]

•   Bypass tagging entirely by creating descriptive notes with all the necessary information.

•   Use a tag like ~MIT! to mark the most important things that you need to do. Change the tag to ~99-Done when you finish with the task or item.

Personal Documents

Time to put your new knowledge about Evernote to work. Let's start with some personal documents as you prepare to move off to college.

I am horrible at maintaining a paper-based filing system. The documents just end up in an unorganized pile. Trying to find something in a hurry is impossible.

Locating needed files has been much easier once I started to scan documents to Evernote. These files are wherever I am. Remember, you can always encrypt them for added security.

1. Create a personal documents notebook stack.

2. Create notebooks for the different document collections.

3. Pull together all the documents you are going to add to Evernote in one place.

4. Upload these documents into your inbox.

5. Begin your organizing process by adding proper titles, merging notes, adding tags, and removing notes no longer beneficial.

6. Change the notebook for the note when you have finished updating it. [10]

I scanned thousands of documents into my Evernote when I was getting ready to move. It took me a couple of months to organize all those documents. It may seem like a long time, but I had uploaded hundreds of papers and I was working on it a little at a time. The benefit was I did not have to carry those documents across the country.

Here are some documents to consider storing in Evernote.

Emergency Notebook

Your emergency notebook is the first notebook to create. This notebook is a place you would store essential documents. These vital documents would include copies of

- identification cards
- emergency contact lists

- copies of legal documents

Don't forget you can encrypt these items for extra security.

Medical Info

Do you know when you were vaccinated and which shots you received? Do you know all the medications you are using? Do you know which drugs are effective for you or not? A medical notebook is a place to store all these different documents. [11] Create a master medical note where you can track injuries, bouts of illness, allergies, etc. It makes filling out medical records at the doctor so much easier. Having this information at your fingertips is a huge time saver. A medical notebook is an excellent place to store any interesting medical-related articles.

Insurance Information

Do you have a life insurance policy? Do you know where it is? Scan a copy and put it in Evernote. You may want to share this notebook with others.

Another useful notebook and master note to create is for an inventory of your major purchases. You can use this inventory during a disaster such as a fire, flood, or other events. [12] You should take pictures of each item and link them to your inventory. One of the great things about Evernote is that it will capture the date when you took the image.

Automobile Information

There are many different items you can store in your automobile notebook. For example, you can keep a copy of your insurance, registration, and license plate. I was visiting a college, and I needed to give them my license plate number. I regret not having a copy of my license plate in my Evernote because the walk back to my car was rather long.

You may also want to keep a digital copy of your owner's manual. This comes in handy when you are chasing down parts.

I will snap a picture of the location where I parked when I am doing a lot of traveling, such as when I park in an airport parking lot. It has helped me on more than one occasion to find my car again. You can delete this picture later when it is no longer needed.

Personal Mementos

A lot can change when you leave for college. Your parents may start to declutter your room. In Evernote, you can store personal documents you want to keep, such as old letters and memories. I have lost a lot of artifacts I wished I kept during moves.

Journal/Diary/Commonplace Book/Bullet Journal

Some people use Evernote to record their thoughts. These thoughts may be in a journal, diary, commonplace book, or bullet journal. These different examples serve the same purpose—record things you want to remember.

Commonplace books are more focused on collecting quotes, tracking what you are reading, reflecting on lessons learned, and writing ideas. [13] Commonplace books were paper notebooks. It so happens that you can integrate a paper notebook with Evernote. Combining paper and digital makes it easier to locate information over time.

A bullet journal is useful for tracking things that need completing. I use my bullet journal to track what occurs in meetings and what I am learning.

Evernote provides the flexibility and capability to curate information regardless of what and why you are saving the information. You should have a notebook dedicated to curating essential information. The key to a successful journal is adding notes to it.

One of my regrets is not starting a journal earlier in my life. It has been rewarding to go back over my recent journaling efforts. I can see how my thought processes have changed. "Keep a journal if you can. It's great to be able to go back and see how you've progressed over the years." [14]

Receipts

Another essential notebook to create is for receipts. You should scan the receipt and place it in this notebook when you make a significant purchase. You should also store the serial numbers and model numbers for these major purchases.

One strategy I have started to employ is having receipts sent to Evernote. I have set up a series of rules in my Gmail account to forward receipts to Evernote. The receipts go to my inbox. I will then process them like other notes.

Software Keys/Codes/Passwords

Adding software to your computer or mobile device often comes with a software activation code. Have you ever lost these codes? I have. Losing activation codes makes reinstallation a pain. Evernote is a convenient place to store these codes. I have a notebook dedicated to all these codes. Ensure that you give them a meaningful title.

Software codes are not the only tech-related items you can store in Evernote. You can also save the connection information for your WiFi and MiFi.[15] I have had to reset my network and computers a few times. This information helped get me back online quicker.

Have you ever forgotten the combination of a combination lock? Store the number in Evernote. I also saved the passcode for my garage door.

There is a lot of other information you can store in Evernote. I use Evernote to track all the applications and add-ons I use in case I have to rebuild a computer system, browser, website, etc.:

- Track plug-ins for different WordPress sites along with passcodes.
- Track extensions for browsers.
- List software applications loaded on computers.

You can also use it to collect game cheat codes and hacks, software instructions, and shortcut key codes.[16]

Equipment Details and Manuals

Have you ever been out shopping and remembered you need to pick up toner, but you couldn't remember what printer you have? It is a pain to have to run home to get the information. It has happened to me on more than one occasion. I now have fewer repeat trips since I use Evernote to track this kind of information.

For example, I needed to do a tune-up on my lawnmower. I took pictures of different parts and pieces including the makes and models. I wanted to ensure I picked up the right parts. I am happy to report that I made only one trip to the store.

You should use Evernote to track when you purchased an item, where you bought it from, and how much it cost. Link to the receipt.

Evernote is an excellent repository for owner manuals, parts lists, and other technical instructions. You should link the manual to your receipt. You can retrieve it from Evernote when and where you need it.

Gift Ideas

You can track more than the equipment details with Evernote. You can keep track of gift ideas. Try to track as many details as possible to make your shopping experience easier. One example is storing clothing sizes. I can never remember my sizes much less than anyone else. I store the clothing and jewelry sizes for my parents, my significant other, and my siblings just in case I want to pick them up gifts. You should also note favorite brands and colors. This note is an ever-changing list.

Dorm Life

Take pictures of typical dorm rooms so you can start planning for moving in. Ensure you also note the dimensions of your room. These pictures and dimensions will help you better plan your move.

Also, take the time to take pictures of the condition of your dorm room before you move in. These will help speed up leaving your room at the end of the year. Record any changes you make to the room in Evernote.

Use these concepts when you later move into a rental or buy your own home. Evernote is a useful place to track repairs and upgrades when it's time to do some home repairs. My wife tracks paint colors so she can get the right color when she needs to do touch-ups or repainting. These notes will help when it comes time to move out or sell.

Note the makes and models of appliances just in case you need to get replacement parts. You should jot down any special instructions you need to make repairs.

Wrap Up

At this point, you should be able to create notebooks and notebook stacks. You should also be able to create different types of notes. It's your turn. Take a moment to run Evernote through its paces. Use Evernote to collect documents you will need on hand while at college. Take time to develop practices to add content to Evernote on a regular basis.

I tried to provide ways you can get the most out of Evernote. I am sure you will discover ways I have not considered.

Pay particular attention to creating good titles and adding appropriate tags. Things are going to start getting busier as you move to college.

***

1. Samuel, Alexandra. Work Smarter with Evernote. Harvard Business School Publishing Corporation, 2013.

2. Collins, Brandon. The 2 Hour Guide to Mastering Evernote - Including: Tips, Uses, and Evernote Essentials. 2nd ed. Future Prophet Publishing LLC, 2012.

3. "Using Evernote to Save Your Schooling," GearFire - Tips for Students, accessed October 13, 2017, http://www.gearfire.net/evernote-school/.

4. Adam. "My Tribute to Evernote: A Student's Guide." Accessed November 21, 2017. http://theflannelboard.blogspot.com/2012/03/my-tribute-to-evernote-students-guide.html.

5. Sinkov, Andrew. "Emailing Into Evernote Just Got Better." Evernote Blog (blog), March 16, 2010. https://blog.evernote.com/blog/2010/03/16/emailing-into-evernote-just-got-better/.

6. Collins, The 2 Hour Guide to Mastering Evernote - Including.

7. "Using Evernote to Save Your Schooling."

8. The Cafe Scholar. "How to Use Evernote to Organize Research » The Cafe Scholar," July 24, 2017. https://www.thecafescholar.com/use-evernote-organize-research/.

9. Collins, The 2 Hour Guide to Mastering Evernote - Including.

10. Ibid.

11. "10 Tips for Using Evernote to De-Stress College from Student Ambassador Megan Cotter," Evernote Blog, April 18, 2012, https://blog.evernote.com/blog/2012/04/18/10-tips-for-using-evernote-to-de-stress-college-from-student-ambassador-megan-cotter/.

12. Collins, The 2 Hour Guide to Mastering Evernote - Including.

13. Pipes, Taylor. "Taking Note: What Commonplace Books Can Teach Us about Our Past." Evernote Blog (blog), February 26, 2016. https://blog.evernote.com/blog/2016/02/26/taking-note-what-commonplace-books-can-teach-us-about-our-past/.

14. Frank, Thomas. "42 College Tips I Learned Freshman Year." College Info Geek, March 4, 2011. https://collegeinfogeek.com/42-things-i-learned-freshman-year/.

15. Collins, The 2 Hour Guide to Mastering Evernote - Including.

16. Ibid.

Chapter Four

To Do Lists and Checklists

All right, all right, all right! It is time to head off to college. It is a marvelous feeling to head off to the unknown. Are you ready?

There are so many things to plan. Evernote is by your side to help - if you let it. You can build checklists to help with all the details. A moving list helps ensure you did not leave anything behind. Evernote will help you complete all the things you need to do once you arrive. Take time to scour the internet for tips and tricks to make your transition smoother. You can add everything you discover to Evernote.

In this chapter, you are going to learn about creating **checklists, linked notes, master notes**, and **contact lists**. You will also learn about using the **Web Clipper** and **sharing notes** and **notebooks**. Let's get started with checklists.

Checklists and To-do Lists

Your brain is mighty but has limitations. Your brain reaches capacity at a certain point and begins to fail. We start to forget to do things. Forgetting leads to missed opportunities and poor relations with others. David Allen, the author of *Getting Things Done* said, "Your mind is for having ideas, not holding them."

Evernote can be your digital brain. You should offload tasks from your memory on a regular basis to Evernote so you can focus on more important things.

Your move to college will not be as smooth or stress-free without a useful checklist. Evernote has a powerful and easy-to-use checklist feature.

You have many things to do for all your classes. You also have tasks to complete for other programs in which you take part. Creating checklists and to-do lists is crucial to keep on track.

You can add a checkbox within your note when you create it. You can check or uncheck the box as appropriate to your task. You can have many checkboxes in a note. You can create a checklist or list with these checkboxes to track tasks, assignments, or other items.

Power tip. You can search through your notes for items you have not checked off. Use the search term **todo:*** (include the asterisk) to see if a note has a checkbox. Search for **todo:true** if you want to find notes for checkboxes that you have checked. Likewise, you would search for **todo:false** if you want to search for the things you still have to do. Save these ToDo searches to your shortcuts list. It makes finding tasks you still need to complete easy.

Linking Notes

You may find notes related to each other as you continue to add them. You may want to solidify these relationships by linking from one note to another. You can do this with note links.

Here are some reasons to create links to notes:

* Create master documents for projects.

* Create master notes for meetings and required tasks.

* Create a master homework assignment list that has checkboxes and links to the details of each assignment.

Here is how you can link one note to another:

1. Right-click on the note in the **Notes List**.

2. Click on **Copy internal link**.

3. Select **Copy app link**.

4. Open the note where you wish to place the link.

5. Paste the note link.

Evernote will insert the title of the linked note along with a hyperlink back to the note.

You can also paste the link in other applications such as email messages and websites. Ensure the note is shareable if you are going to paste a link for others to view the note. You will learn about sharing notes later in this chapter. The link for the note will go to the original note if you share the link on the internet. Everyone will be able to see the updates when you update the note.

Creating Dynamic Checklists

Let's combine the power of checklists and linking notes. Imagine that you are taking an English class. You have just uploaded your syllabus and all your handouts to your English notebook in Evernote. One of the first notes you will want to create is an assignment list.

Add all your assignments to this assignment list note along with the dates they are due. Add a checkbox before each of the assignments. You now have a checklist on which you can check off assignments as you complete them.

You can make this checklist more useful by linking to each of your assignment sheets. Find the assignment sheet in Evernote, right-click on it, and copy the internal link. Go back to your assignment checklist, highlight the assignment, and insert the link. You can also link to assignment instructions on the web.

Searching for open checkboxes will alert you to uncompleted assignments. You now have a dynamic checklist that will allow you to navigate to assignment instructions with ease.

Master Notes

You can increase the level of organization for your notes by creating a master note. This note links to other notes. You could create a master note from your assignment list that links to the description of each assignment.

This type of note will help you find things easier.

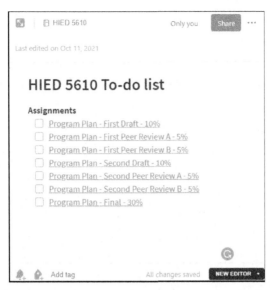

Figure 7. Example of a master note linking to individual assignments.

Creating a Master Note

You will hand curate the links you want to include in your note. For example, you will often have a list of subtasks if you have a project. You can create a note for each of the subtasks with the details. You will then place a link to this detailed subtask note on your master project note. Here is how you do it:

1. Navigate to the complete subtask note.

2. Copy a shareable link to your clipboard using the process for creating a shareable link.

3. Return to the master note and paste the link in the location that best serves your needs.

4. Repeat until you have all your notes linked to a master note for the project.

You can use a master note for many different reasons. Here are some ideas for their use:

• Create a master note to manage the steps for a major project.

• Create a master note for all the assignments and worksheets you have for one of your classes.

• Create a master note for all the checklists you create.

Lists

One of the more useful reasons I have for using Evernote is the creation of lists. I maintain many different lists in Evernote. It allows me to have them with me all the time. I can refer to them wherever I am. Lists make it easy to check items once I find something I need or complete a task. Here are some of the ways I use lists, along with some other ideas.

To-Do Lists

I maintain a master to-do list. It is not for projects, which have their own lists. The master to-do list is to track the various things I need to do during my day. I will put a task on this list every time I think of something I need to do. I have a link to this list from my shortcuts. I check the tasks off as I complete them. I duplicate the to-do list, remove completed tasks, and switch out the link on my shortcuts at the end of the week.

My list has three major sections that span two columns. The three sections are work, home, and my side hustle. Each item has a checkbox so I can check things off. There are links to other notes with more details when appropriate. I will navigate to the individual notes and add the tag "99-done" when I have completed that task. "99-done" is my tag for completed items. I can search for things that are not done, such as blog posts I want to write.

Remember to create a shortcut to a search query for "todo" items. This search query will show you anything open. This query is especially useful if you have many lists with checkboxes.

Moving Lists

I planned my entire move in Evernote during my last move across the country. The list made the move so much easier. I tailored my moving checklist based on a lot of other moving checklists, as well as on my needs. Each item had a checkbox I could check off once I completed a task.

Evernote can also be a great help when looking for a new place to live. You can use the Web Clipper to clip new listings that you like so that you can compare them.

Grocery List

My grocery list is another one of my most-used lists. I have a master list of all the grocery items I usually buy. I will put a check in the checkbox when I am deciding what to buy and uncheck the box when I pick up the item in the store. Grocery shopping is over when you clear all the boxes. The list resets itself for the next time you need it.

Coupons and Offers

Another useful notebook that you can create is for coupons and offers. You can then create a master coupon note that links to the different coupons and offers you collected. I would recommend putting an expiration date next to the item so you know when to discard it.

Restaurants

Take a moment to scan copies of menus for your favorite restaurants. You can create a list of the restaurants and arrange them by type of food. It saves a lot of time when you are starving.

Shopping Wish List

When you are browsing online stores or even window shopping, you can save a note by typing it in, taking photos, or using the Web Clipper to move it into a wish list notebook. You can then link to these notes in a master wish list note. You can refer to this list when you are shopping. You can also make your wish list notebook public and share it with others.

Home Inventory

I have discussed taking inventory pictures for insurance purposes. Inventories can serve other purposes. It can help keep you from purchasing duplicate items. I use my home inventory list to find books, CDs, and movies. I take pictures of my bookshelves and the shelves with my music CDs and movies. The title of the note is the location of the shelf.

I can search Evernote to see if I already own a book or movie and its location. Evernote will search through each picture and let me know where I can find a book or movie.

Numbers to Remember

Evernote is an excellent backup to your memory. Everyone keeps phone numbers on their phone, unfortunately, I have seen people lose their phone and all their contacts. They have to ask everyone to send them their phone numbers when they are setting up their new phone. You lose a lot of essential numbers in this transition. Evernote can provide a secondary location for numbers, especially if you build out contact notes.

Contacts & Networking

You will interact with many different people while in college. Your success in life is dependent upon your interactions and relationships with others. You can increase your success by remembering details of your interactions. Evernote allows you to track these exchanges. You can store and retrieve information about the last time you spoke with someone. This contact information will help you restart the conversation and make it more personal. Let's discuss ways you can use Evernote to improve personal relations.

Contact notebook

Begin by creating a contacts notebook. You should have a separate note for each contact in this notebook. Create a meaningful title for the note, such as using the individual's name. It is up to you whether you want to go with the first name, then last name, or last name then first. It is beneficial to be consistent. This contact note will be your master file on the individual. It is a place where you include all the essential details you learn about the person. Create a unique tag for this individual. I use a semicolon to identify contact tags, for example, ":Skrabut-Stan". Use this tag with other notes related to this individual.

Basic contact information

Here are some suggestions for content to put in your master note:

- Name
- Title
- Business
- Email address

- Phone numbers

- Business card – Evernote allows you to do this with its document image capability. The business card is then searchable.

- Personal information – Add information about them and their families such as birthdays and anniversaries.

- Other information to help remember them.

- Other information that you can use to help them. For example, what issues are they working on or problems they are trying to solve [1]

- Web-based content such as their LinkedIn profile.

Contact Log

There are two ways you can approach maintaining a contact log for your contacts. You can keep notes in your master contact note or link to other notes. You can also do a combination of both methods.

Master Contact Note

You can keep track of all your interactions on a master contact note for the individual. You will want to record any communications, for example, phone calls, email messages, face-to-face meetings, etc. You can insert a date stamp by pressing Shft+Alt+D when you are using the desktop version of Evernote. [2] These keyboard shortcuts increase productivity.

Link Out to Notes

The other way you can build out your master contact list is to create a separate note and link out to it from your master contact note. You can also add a date stamp if that is important to you. Include the contact tag for the individual as another way to create a connection to the separate notes.

Use reminders to help stay in touch to increase the usefulness of your contact notes. [3] You can also sort these notes based on when you last updated them. You can then see when it is time to reach out to one of your contacts. You can refer to a select set of notes last updated during a specific period.

Wrap Up

You can make your move a lot smoother and stress-free if you use Evernote to build moving checklists. These checklists can help you identify groceries you need to buy, things you need for your room, and tasks you need to complete.

When you move to your new college environment, you will meet new people. Evernote is an excellent tool for creating a lasting contact list. You can take advantage of lessons from the business world by recording interactions with those you meet. You never know how it may help you in the future.

You will be going to your first college class in a couple of days. Starting classes is when the real power of Evernote will become clear. Time to settle in, the real work is about to begin.

***

---

1. Ward, David. Evernote for Lawyers: A Guide to Getting Organized & Increasing Productivity. The Attorney Marketing Center, n.d.
2. Ibid.
3. Ibid.

Chapter Five

First Day of Classes

Today is a big day—your first day of classes! Are you ready? While Evernote is going to prove to be a great sidekick, you are going to have to work hard. I will not only be showing you how to use Evernote to support your learning, but I am also going to share success tips along the way. For example, to be successful in college, you should attend all your classes, if possible, even the 8 a.m. classes. Showing up is vital. Learning takes place through dialogue—dialogue with the content, fellow students, and your instructor.[1] Dialogue means that you have to be present.

In this chapter, we are going to focus on setting goals, taking class notes, building a homework planner, and creating book notes. I think Evernote's capabilities will surprise you. Let's get started.

Setting Your Academic Goals

Establishing short-term and long-term goals and documenting them in Evernote is another valuable tip to help you succeed. Completing your degree is one long goal. Break this large goal into smaller manageable goals. You should also create some short-term goals based on how well you want to finish a semester or a specific course.[2] For example, you could set a goal to attend every class session. Make it a goal to study for at least 30 minutes each day. This will help you become more successful in your classes. Other goals include completing a certificate program in your specialty, maintaining a specific GPA, completing your degree on time, learning a language, publishing an academic paper, serving in a leadership position, taking on an internship, and more.[3] Right now, the goal is to get through your first day.

You can achieve amazing things if you set your mind to it. Research has shown that you will have greater success in achieving your goals if you write them down. Evernote is a great place to write down your goals and the progress you are making towards them.

I like the strategy that Michael Hyatt outlined in his article, "How Evernote can Help you Achieve Your Goals in 2015."[4]

1. Create a master note of all the goals you want to do in the academic year. You may also create a master note of all the goals that you want to do in life. Each of your goals should be a Smart goal (Specific, Measurable, Attainable, Realistic, Timebound).

2. Prepare a separate note for each of your goals. This is where you will write the specific details of the goal. Use tags to define it as a goal and the year for the goal. Set a reminder for the note. Hyatt also has sections for Key Motivations, Next Actions, Progress Reports, and Random Notes. He has created a template to make this easier to complete.

3. Link each note to the master goal note.

4. Create a saved search to goal and year tags. Save the search to your shortcuts.

You should now have a system to help keep you on track to meeting your goals. It is up to you to use this strategy.

Taking Class Notes

You are going to attend many classes and take lots of notes. These classes may be face-to-face or online. You may also pursue learning opportunities through massively open online courses (MOOCs) or through sites like LinkedIn Learning. Regardless, Evernote is a great place to collect your notes.

Use Evernote for your note-taking. You will have your notes with you wherever you go.

Let's set you up for success. Create a notebook stack for your courses. Make a separate notebook for each course in this stack. Remember, click on the "+" plus sign when you move your cursor over the **Notebooks** tool and give the notebook a name. You can speed up this process by using the key combination Alt+Shft+N. Next, create a new note for each class period. You can add your notes, upload PDFs, collect screen captures, add slide decks and other files, etc. to the notebook. [5] Refer to Chapter Three to see the many ways to create a note. But now, click on the **New Note** button and begin typing to start a basic text note. Pressing the key combination Alt+Ctrl+N is a quicker way to create a note. Ensure the note is in your course notebook so you can find it much quicker. Titling your note and adding tags will help you find it easier.

Additionally, generate a master course note for your class. Add links to it from all the other notes in your notebook. A master course note will help organize your notes. It is a practice that will serve you as you later manage projects and research activities.

There are different ways to start and take notes. Let's explore these different methods. These methods build upon the capture methods outlined in the previous chapter.

Text Notes

A simple text note is the most natural place to start. Just open Evernote and start a note. Type in your key points and information. This note will be your rough draft. Create a link by right-clicking on the note in the Notes List and click on **Copy internal link** then select the **Copy app link**. Add it to your class master note by pasting the note link.

I have found my in-class notes are quite rough. I flesh them out when I look at them at the end of the day. Reviewing your notes at the end of the day is essential. You can add more detail to them as well as link to worksheets, add images, or provide other enhancements. These improvements will help when it is time to study. You can also add references your professor mentioned and embed them into your notes as text or images.

You may want to consider using a template as a starting point for your notes. The Cornell note template is an excellent starting point. I would like to take a moment to tell you about templates.

Templates

A template is a great tool to help increase productivity and a great way to get started on a note. It lets me know what I need to include in the note, saving me time and mental energy.

You can create templates based on a note-taking format you like. You can also use templates that others create. You will find quite a variety if you search the internet for "Evernote templates."

You may have templates for different types of notes you want to create. For example, you may use the Cornell method template for your class notes and a meeting template for your different meetings.

Create a notebook for all your templates as soon as possible. Next, copy in a template someone else has created or design your own template. Take time to design it the way you want it to look. You can use color, tables, images, etc. to get started. Make a copy of the template, rename it, and move it to a template notebook when you need to use it.

Evernote has a directory of different templates you can save and change. They cover a wealth of topics from planning and goal setting to travel and marketing. Here are the major categories at https://Evernote.com/templates.

- Creative Writing

- Getting Things Done® (GTD)

- Home and Garden

- Management Resources

- Marketing & Sales

- Meetings

- Party Planning

- Personal Well-being

- Project Management

- School

- Travel

These different templates will help you be more productive. Over time, you will put together a collection of templates to help with meetings, budgets, planning, goals, projects, note-taking, and much more.

Remember, all the functionality of Evernote is at your fingertips when you create your template. You can link to other notes. You can link to different templates and documents. For example, you can link to a budget or timeline from your planning template.[6] Update the links in your notes after you copy and start your new note.

Cornell Template

You can start your note from a blank note, but I recommend you create your note with a Cornell note template. The Cornell note helps capture critical points of a lecture. You can get a copy of this template here (https://evernote.com/templates/cornell-notes).

The Cornell note template has three major sections: cue-column, note-taking column, and summary. The note-taking column is for recording notes for the class. The cue column is for generating key questions about your notes and the class. Finally, use the summary section to sum up your notes.

Here are some key things you will want to include in your note:

• Take pictures of any slides or whiteboards relevant to the lecture. You can paste them into your notes.

• Upload handouts into Evernote and link to them in your notes.

• Capture audio clips and link to them in your notes. Sound clips are great for capturing foreign language pronunciations, music classes, necessary speeches, key definitions, quotes, etc.[7]

Handwritten Notes

You may prefer handwriting your notes in class. Perhaps your professor will not allow digital devices in the classroom. You will need to handwrite notes in both cases. Don't worry. Handwriting is an excellent strategy for taking notes. It may be better than typing your notes in class.[8]

You can capture notes you have written on a piece of paper, in your notebook, or on a whiteboard, just to name a few. These notes become searchable once you add them to Evernote. Evernote can search through different types of documents. It can even search through handwritten notes. You now enjoy the best of both worlds: paper and digital.

Capturing Handwritten Notes

Let's look at different ways you can enter handwritten notes into Evernote. The method you use is dependent on where you write the note. Scan the note into Evernote if it is single pieces of paper. Use the Evernote camera if the note is in a bound notebook like a bullet journal or on a whiteboard. In case you are not familiar with bullet journaling, it is a note-taking strategy using a physical notebook. You can also create a handwritten note using Evernote's handwriting tool. There are other tools like Penultimate, which works with Evernote.

Scanning Notes. A scanner is a great way to capture notes written on loose leaves of paper. I have a desktop scanner called ScanSnap, which is a workhorse, especially if you do a lot of scanning. It will scan documents to Evernote. When I moved from Wyoming to New York, I spent days scanning all my papers into Evernote. This collection took up four large filing cabinets.

You can install a scanner application on your mobile device if you do not have access to a desktop scanner. I use a program called Handy Scanner, but there are many other scanners. You can also use the Evernote camera if you want to capture a document with your phone.

Evernote Camera. The Evernote camera is often the quickest way to capture a written note. Start a new note, click on the camera button, and take the picture. Evernote will detect the edges of the note and recognize it as a document.

Moleskine Notebooks. I am a huge fan of Moleskine notebooks. Moleskine creates high-quality journals in which you can handwrite your notes and add drawings. Evernote has partnered with Moleskine to integrate the analog and digital world. Evernote adds tags and notebooks to a scanned note based on smart stickers. Search the internet for the process to change smart sticker attributes because Evernote is currently making changes to its apps.

The result is that individual pages are searchable documents. I only use Moleskine notebooks. Besides being a durable notebook with quality paper, I also enjoy the connection with Evernote. I have increased my productivity of using Evernote and the Moleskine notebook in combination through a note-taking technique called bullet journaling. Scanning your notes to Evernote allows you to get the best of both worlds if you love to write in a notebook.

Scanning a Notebook Page. Capturing a page to your notebook is not difficult. Open your journal flat and place the string bookmark between the two pages. Many different types of physical notebooks have a string to help mark a place in the notebook. Evernote uses this string marker to delineate the pages. Start the Evernote camera tool on your mobile device. Set the camera to document camera. Focus the camera over one of the pages, and Evernote will capture the page. Then, focus the camera on the next page if there are more pages. Repeat until you have taken pictures of all the pages for that section. Add a title to the note and save it. Later, you can go back and add tags and place it in the appropriate notebook. I recommend batching your processing if you have many pages to capture.

I will capture all my pages to Evernote at the end of each month. The reason I wait until the end of the month is in large part due to bullet journaling. You should capture your written note pages more often because of your accelerated status as a student.

Handwriting Applications

Several handwriting applications work together with Evernote. One of my favorite programs is Penultimate. Penultimate allows you to capture handwritten notes. Evernote also has a natural handwriting capability. On your mobile device, you have to select the handwriting tool.

Penultimate. Penultimate is an iPad application that allows you to create handwritten notes and drawings. You can then export the files directly into Evernote. As expected, these are searchable with Evernote.

Penultimate is more than a blank screen on which to write. You can choose from a wide array of paper styles to include lines, dots, and grids to calendars, planners, and to-do lists. There are other paper collections you can buy such as music paper, young writer's paper collection, and photo album paper. You can also change the formatting of the pen to increase thickness, change color, and turn it into a highlighter. There is also a cut and paste feature to allow you to move text around the screen.

I recommend you invest in a fine point stylus for your iPad to get the most out of Penultimate. My experience improved with an appropriate pen.

Evernote Handwriting. There are different ways to access the handwriting feature in Evernote. You can start writing with an Android device by selecting the handwriting option when starting the note. You can access the handwriting or sketch feature for a note on an iOS device by selecting the tool at the bottom of the note.

Strategies for Using Handwritten Notes

Capturing anything is one of the superpowers of Evernote. You can record writing and find it later with a search. The clarity of the writing will determine if you can find it in a search. You can also select the language you want to use for your search. Evernote can identify 28 typewritten and 11 handwritten languages.

Here are some ideas for using your handwritten notes:

• Write your notes and then take a picture of them if you are not allowed to use computers or mobile devices in your classroom.

• Organize your handwritten notes with all your other notes for a class or activity.

• Take pictures of your notes often rather than let them pile up. I mark the corner of my notes so I know I have scanned them or I throw them away because I have a digital copy.

• "Use the library scanner to scan important content related to classes or research projects. Scan documents to PDF files that can be easily added to Evernote." [9]

• Set the file location for your scanner to go to Evernote. Ensure your scanner has this capability when you buy it.

• Take time to tag your notes, give them proper titles, and organize them in notebooks after you scan or photograph your handwritten pages.

- Transcribe your notes on your computer as an added studying tactic. [10]

- "Take smart notes. Find a note-taking system that works well for you, and focus on learning rather than simply recording the information." [11]

Taking Pictures

Taking pictures is another great way to capture important information. Not only can you capture an image of an object, you can also search through images. Evernote will recognize text in pictures that match your search query because of built-in OCR.

I will take photos of the presentation slides, whiteboard notes, or easel annotations when I go to conferences or meetings. Take pictures of whiteboards in your classes and meetings to capture the conversation. You can later search through the whiteboard annotations.

Taking pictures of the contents is a helpful classroom strategy. You can go back later and type in more notes. You can also take notes at the same time you are taking pictures. You can then mark up your photos with more information using a program like Skitch (More about Skitch later in this chapter).

Strategies for Pictures in Evernote

- Ensure you provide appropriate titles, tags, and notebooks soon after the class while the information is fresh in your mind.

- Share your detailed notes with others.

- Capture images of whiteboards or essential slides. You can focus on the lesson rather than writing everything down.

- Annotate your images and PDF documents with programs like Skitch.

- Take a picture of your art project and save it to Evernote if you don't want to keep a physical copy of it.

- "Take pictures of things that cannot be scanned. Evernote allows you to search through the text of an image." [12]

- Capture pictures of images, sketches, and other drawings.

• Use a bookstand or book clip to keep the book open if you need to take pictures of a book. [13]

Annotating Images and PDFs

You can increase the usefulness of your images and PDFs by annotating them. You can use annotations to label parts of a picture or add notes to a document. Skitch is a powerful tool for making notes on images.

Annotating Images With Skitch

I use Skitch almost daily. The version I have is an application for the desktop, which is still available for Macs and iOS products. Skitch is now part of Evernote.

You can use Skitch to annotate images and PDF files. Annotating means you can add arrows, text, boxes, circles, and lines to an image or PDF. You can also write on the object with a marker or highlighter. Add stamps to an image or PDF to show rejected, attention, question, approved, and perfect. You can also pixelate parts of an image as well as crop it. Finally, you can change the color and thickness of the annotations that you make.

I often use Skitch to capture screenshots and mark them up with the desktop version. The version within Evernote will not allow you to capture screenshots, but you will be able to mark up what you do capture.

How to Use Skitch. Begin by selecting the note with the picture or PDF you want to annotate. Selecting a note will display the note in the note view frame. Right-click on the image or PDF and select the **Annotate This PDF/Image** option. You can also make a copy of the image or PDF for annotating.

Ideas for Using Skitch. You can use Skitch for image annotation to add emphasis or clarity to an artifact. Here are some examples to consider:

• Take pictures of different organisms and annotate the different parts as part of a biology course.

• Annotating countries, rivers, cities, etc., would be appropriate for a geography course.

- Annotation would be appropriate to identify nomenclature if you are working with mechanical devices.

- Use the Skitch tools to critique a document, webpage, or image.

- Take a picture of a whiteboard and add additional annotations to add clarity.

Sharing with others is one of the great benefits of annotating images and documents.

PDFs

There are many benefits to adding PDF documents to Evernote. You can use tools like Skitch to add annotations to the PDFs as a way to call attention to important parts. You can also search through the text found in the PDF. Searching text is a powerful capability. The PDF search capability is available with a personal or business subscription.

Evernote scans the text with its OCR capability when you add a PDF document to Evernote. Here are some tips to achieve greater success.

- Scanned documents need clear, typed text.

- The document must be less than 100 pages long and less than 25 Mb in size.

- The documents cannot be corrupted or unreadable. Additionally, they cannot be password protected.

The PDF search capability also allows you to search PDF documents scanned without OCR functionality. You can scan in documents with your school's copiers and scanner, your scanner, or even a mobile scanner.

Saving your PDFs to Evernote will provide you with 24/7 access. Additionally, you will be able to search through them as well as annotate them. You can also write your comments and ideas on the note because you are attaching the PDF to a note. Increase the value of your PDF textbooks by annotating them.

Handouts

You will often receive handouts for your different classes. The handouts may be something you need to read or they may be homework instructions. They may be digital or paper. You may receive them in an email, a link from your learning management system, or you may download them from some other site. Your teacher may hand them out in class.

The first thing you will want to do is ensure you have a digital copy on your computer regardless of how you received your handout. You may have to scan the handout to get a digital copy. You will then upload the handouts to your Evernote account. I recommend making it a unique note. Organize the handouts where they make the most sense. Place PDFs in your course or activity notebook. Copy the link to the note and include it in your course's master note or course note as appropriate.

Wrapping Up the End of the Day

You should have a collection of notes at the end of the day—one note for each class you attended. The end of the day is an excellent time to name and organize everything you collect. It is also an excellent time to create the links that tie all the notes together. You will thank me when it comes time to study! Speaking of studying, let's put together a plan for organizing your homework.

Homework Planner

Your instructors expect you to prove that you are grasping the content as the classes progress. They envision you will read the articles, chapters, and other documents they assign. They want you to complete assignments, prepare presentations, and work on projects. You can become overwhelmed in a short time if you do not have a plan. You will have hundreds of assignments across your time in college. Your brain can keep only so many things in short-term memory. Evernote comes in handy to overcome this issue. "A key to success in college is to schedule every moment of your day, even free time, so you are making the most of your time—especially during that first year when you might be new to making your own scheduling choices."[14]

A homework planner enables you to track all the different things you need to complete. You should never hand in late homework if you have a productive homework system. A homework planner tracks your deadlines and homework schedule. First, create a master to-do list for each class in Evernote. Each task should be a separate note. These notes should include detailed instructions on how to finish each homework assignment. You should have a link to each of the instruction notes with a checkbox to mark it off when complete. The title of the note should include the date it is due using the yearmoda date format. You should also set a reminder in Evernote appropriate for you to meet the deadline. Add these master to-do lists to your favorites so you can access them with ease. You do not want to turn in late assignments.

Your professor will often hand out a course syllabus on the first day of class. The course syllabus outlines what you need to do and when you need to have it done. The syllabus will form the basis of your homework planner. Take time to build out your homework planner system as soon as you receive the syllabus. The course schedule can serve as the foundation of your master to-do list for that particular class.

Lists

Homework master to-do lists are not the only lists you are going to want to create. Evernote is an excellent tool for creating all types of lists. In the previous chapter, I suggested you use Evernote to create to-do lists, moving lists, grocery lists, shopping wish lists, home inventories, restaurant lists, and coupon lists. I am now going to provide other list ideas to improve your quality of life. I wish I had created many of these lists when I first ventured out on my own. I now appreciate their value.

Booklist

You can create a simple booklist to track the books you want to read. Add a checkbox to each book and mark off each book as you have read it. You can take it to another level by capturing notes about the books you read and linking them to your master booklist. Take a picture of the book and add it to your booklist if you want to ensure you are getting the right book. I am always adding new books to my lists as I discover them from friends, podcasts, or other publications. Having an updated list on hand when going into a bookstore makes it easy to see if you have a book before buying it. You can add the release date of a book that has not yet been published to your list.

Take a picture of someone's bookshelf if you are looking for reading ideas. [15] You can then search Evernote for a book title and discover where you had last seen it.

You can also automate your book capturing process. You can have a new note created for every *New York Times* bestseller by using If This Then That (IFTTT). [16] You will never run out of best-selling books. IFTTT is an automation strategy that I will explain in more detail in Chapter Eight.

You may also want to create a booklist just for the classes you are taking. It is also crucial to capture the ISBNs of the books so you can search for the best prices for the books.

Reading Lists

You can also create lists to track articles, blog posts, and other documents you want to read. Link to the documents and articles both in and out of Evernote. You can link to articles you uploaded to Evernote. You can clip webpages into a "read later" notebook with the Web Clipper and link to them in your reading lists. Uploading the articles makes reading them convenient while you are commuting, traveling, or waiting.

Sometimes, your professors or college departments will create reading lists around a specific discipline. Add these reading lists to Evernote. These academic professionals are pointing you in the right direction.

Books, Movies, and Music

I have separate lists for books I want to read, movies I want to see, and new songs and bands I want to explore. I also use lists to track applications I want to try out and podcast episodes to which I want to listen. If something new is coming out and it looks interesting, I put it on one of my lists. In some cases, I may see a poster of an event I want to take in. I will take a picture of the advertisement. [17] I have a quick list of ideas to pursue when it is time to kick back and relax.

Additionally, I have a list of blog posts I want to write, podcast episodes I want to create, and videos I want to record.

Vocabulary List

A vocabulary list for all the new words you will be learning in your classes is another list you may want to consider. Each discipline has its own vocabulary. The quicker you learn these words, the more successful you will be in these classes. Add words you find in the books you are reading along with their definitions. Review these words often to make them part of your vocabulary. Your reading skills will improve as your vocabulary grows.

Book Notes

Developing a strong reading habit is one of the more essential activities you should be developing as a college student. The research I did for my book *Read to Succeed: The Power of Books to Transform Your Life and to Put You on the Path to Success* highlighted that successful people have a robust reading habit. You should develop a reading habit also. Find books in your discipline or area of personal interest and start to read them. [18]

The strategies for capturing notes from your books depend on several factors, such as if you own the book or not. I purchased and kept all my schoolbooks. You should keep books related to your specialty because they will serve as the foundation for your professional library. I also believe in marginalia. Marginalia is when you mark up your book by taking notes and underlining key phrases. You should naturally look for the main ideas in a book but also finding quotes, stories, and useful ideas while reading. Here are some successful strategies for capturing notes from your books.

Mark Up Your Book

You can mark up your book if you own your book. I make annotations in the margins and underline key points. You can do the same thing. You can then scan or take pictures of the pages with your annotations and send them to Evernote. Use Skitch to annotate the pages further once the notes are in Evernote.

Create an Index Page

Another strategy you can use when marking up your book is to use the blank pages at the beginning of a book as an index. List quotes, stories, and ideas you note along with the page number. [19] Take a picture of the index e and add it to Evernote. Ensure you take time to provide a useful title and add tags to help find the content later. Evernote will be able to also search through what you have written if your writing is clear.

Building Study Guides With Evernote

SQ3R is an effective strategy for capturing notes to Evernote as you build study guides. SQ3R stands for

- Scan
- Question
- Read
- Recite
- Review

Scan. Take a moment to scan through a new book or chapter before reading it. Get a feel for the book composition. How does the author emphasize different aspects?

Question. This next section is where you start to use Evernote. Add a new note and start asking questions. Write down questions specific to what you will be reading. Turn headings into questions. For example, for this section of this book, you could ask the following questions:

- What are book notes?
- How do you mark up your book?
- How do you capture notes to Evernote with SQ3R?
- What is SQ3R?
- How do you use SQ3R?

Read. Next, you are trying to answer the questions created in the question phase as you read your book. You can write the answers next to your questions. You are now building a study aid.

Recite. Review your questions and try to recite the answers you wrote down. Keep track of the ones you did not get right. These are areas where you will have to brush up.

Review. Go back and review what you got wrong in the recitation step. Repeat the recitation and review process once you have gone through a thorough review.

Craft Your Notes in Evernote and Add Images from Books

This is a slight twist on the note-taking process noted in the SQ3R section. The only difference is that when you see a powerful quote in your book, take a picture of it and add it to your note in the place that makes sense.

Capture Notes With Readwise

I have just learned about a powerful program called Readwise. You can use Readwise to take a picture of a book page and highlight notes. Readwise then uses OCR which converts the notes into editable text. I will explain how I am using Readwise to capture essential notes from the books and articles I am reading in the next section.

Capturing Notes from Kindle

You can export your Kindle notes and highlights from books you read on Kindle devices and save them in Evernote. You can find your highlights at https://read.amazon.com/notebook. You can then use a program called Bookcision or Klib to capture the notes and paste them into an Evernote note.

Another strategy you can use is to capture a screenshot of the Kindle page. I have Kindle running on my iPad. You can capture the screen by pressing the **Home** and **Power** button at the same time. Upload the images into an Evernote note.

You can also use the Web Clipper to capture the highlights and notes from your Kindle page (https://read.amazon.com/notebook) to Evernote. [20]

Use a program like Readwise to transfer your notes and highlights from your Kindle and send them to Evernote on a predetermined schedule. Readwise will append new notes and highlights to the end of the appropriate Evernote note after each note-taking session. I then add selected notes to Zotero, my citation management tool. This strategy has accelerated my research efforts.

Placing these notes into appropriate notebooks related to your course is essential. Give them proper titles and add meaningful tags so you can retrieve them later. One last step is to link the note to other notes and include it in your class master note.

Assorted Homework and Classroom Activities

Your instructors are going to assign different class activities and homework assignments. Use Evernote to prepare for these various activities. Collect research material, draft content, and build your portfolio with Evernote. Let's look at some of the things your instructors will ask you to do.

Discussions

You will have to take part in discussions in face-to-face and online classes. You can sound like a genius if you take a few moments to craft your answers in Evernote first. Jot down the question as well as your answer. Add the combination of the question and answer to your class notes. Also, draft your answers outside of your learning management system using Evernote. Drafting responses outside of the learning management system will prevent you from doing a lot of rework. Nothing is more frustrating than crafting a great response to a question only to have your learning management system go down before you could submit your answer.

Presentations

Evernote is a fantastic support tool for presenters. You will give many presentations while in college and beyond. Evernote is a great tool to set up speaker notes for speeches or presentations. You can collect speaker notes for a specific speech as well as collect information that will help you for future presentations in and out of school. Think about the long-term as you collect your content. You don't want to waste a lot of time sifting through books and articles a second or third time. Save useful examples, quotes, jokes, tweets, statistics, etc. to Evernote anytime you find them.

You should create a presentation stack in Evernote w notebooks:

- Illustrations
- Jokes
- Quotes
- Tweets
- Statistics [21]

Add relevant content to the appropriate notebook as you come across it. Build a library you can use over and over again.

You can create speaking notes with excerpts from these various notebooks. You could have an iPad with your Evernote speaker notes in front of you, or you could print them out. You should also record information about when and where you gave the presentation as well as the audience's response. [22] You can link to each presentation as a quick reference. These references can be useful as you complete resumes, apply for grants, or prepare for other speaking events. The information that you collect while in college will help you after you graduate.

Blogs

You may need to write blog posts either on a personal blog or on a class blog. I started a blog in 2011 as part of a class assignment. I have been contributing to it ever since. Evernote is a great tool to help prepare your blog posts.

Create a notebook to hold all your drafted blog posts. Start with a blog post template so you maintain some consistency from one article to another. A template will also help your writing by letting you know what information you need to capture or write. I use templates for my blogs and podcasts. They prompt me with different elements such as title, keywords, examples, images, etc.

Pull together the resources you need for your blog post in Evernote. Now, it is a matter of drafting your blog post. One of the benefits of having a system like this is that you can work on many different drafts at the same time.

Use different tags to help identify posts as you move through your different draft stages. Copy the content to your blogging platform once the articles are complete.

Eportfolios

An eportfolio is another project instructors may ask you to create. An eportfolio is a repository of artifacts. It is a collection of work you have completed to show what you learned to your instructors. These artifacts could be papers you have written, presentations, posters, works of art, music composed, etc.

Evernote is an excellent tool for creating an eportfolio. You can create an eportfolio notebook stack and organize it into sub-notebooks. Include a note for each artifact. Use each note to explain why you included the object and what you had learned by creating it.

You can use this eportfolio throughout your academic career. You can add and remove objects as it meets your needs. You can use this eportfolio after you finish school and head out into the working world. I include a link to my Evernote eportfolio in my cover letter while I am job hunting.

Try to convince your instructor to let you use an eportfolio you set up in Evernote. Link to notes you have created in the program they want you to use if your instructor requires an eportfolio in a different program.

Sharing Notes and Notebooks

There are times when you may want to share your notes with classmates, instructors, or others on a team. You may desire to share meeting notes, study notes, or other relevant information. You must decide what the recipient can do with your note such as edit the note or just view it. Additionally, can recipients invite others to view or edit the note? You must also determine how many notes you want to share. You can place the documents in a shared notebook if you're going to share several documents. [23]

Sharing Notes

Evernote makes this easy. Right-click on the note from the **Notes List**. Select the **Share** option. At this point, you have to make some decisions.

The three options are:

- Create a shareable link
- Invite someone
- Email a copy

Create a Shareable Link

You can create a shareable link to your note by enabling the link. You can then share the link with others by copying the link to your clipboard and pasting it in other places such as other notes, email messages, or on the web. This level of sharing only provides note viewing.

Invite Someone

Evernote will present a pop-up dialog box where you can enter the contact information for the person to whom you want to send the link. You will have to decide if you wish the individual to view the note, edit the note, or edit the note and be able to invite others to edit the note. These individuals would have to have an Evernote account. The note would show up in their **Shared with Me** section.

Email a Copy

This option will present a simple link from the share dialog box. Clicking on the link will allow you to send a copy of the note contents to a recipient. It is important to note that if you make changes to your note, the email recipient will not be able to view your changes.

You will see a small icon next to the title in the notes list indicating that you shared the note. This icon also appears in the upper right corner of the note. Removing permissions will remove the icon.

Sharing Notebooks

There are times when you will want to share a collection of notes. The easiest way to share various notes is to create a notebook, place notes you want to share into the notebook, and then share the notebook. You will then be able to share everything set in the notebook with everyone who has access to the notebook. Others can also share this notebook if they have editing rights. Having editing rights can be useful when you are working on a group project. You can share your notes and study guides with the entire study group. [24]

You can share a notebook with a single person or more than one person as long as you have their email addresses.

Sharing a notebook is quite easy. Click on the notebook name in the sidebar. Next, click on the **More actions** (three dots) at the top of the notes list, and finally, select **Share notebook**. A dialog box should appear. Enter the name or email address in the field. Decide upon the permissions that you will allow. The options are **Can view**, **Can edit**, and **Can edit and invite**. Finally, click on the **Send Invitation** button.

You can remove access in a similar manner.

Here are some ideas you may want to consider for shared notebooks:

• Are you a teaching assistant or tutor? Create a shared notebook with the instructor or coordinator. You can share lesson plans, worksheets, answer keys, and examples of completed work.

• Working on a group research project? Set up a shared reference notebook and collect all your research into that notebook.

Wrap Up

So, how did your first day go? College is different than high school, isn't it? How did note-taking go? Were you able to get your notes into Evernote? How about your handouts?

You should have a better idea of taking class notes with Evernote, building a homework planner, and creating book notes. This first step will help you be successful in your academic career.

In the next chapter, you will learn strategies for setting up your day for success as well as learn ways to get your notes from Evernote when and where you need them.

***

1. Hansen, Randall. "25 Tips to Help You Survive and Thrive Your Freshman Year." LiveCareer, December 15, 2017. https://www.livecareer.com/resources/jobs/search/first-year-success.

2. Pascarella, Alyssa. "12 Tips to Help You Survive Your Freshman Year of College." RISLA - RI Student Loan Authority, August 11, 2017. https://blog.risla.com/how-to-survive-your-freshman-year-of-college.

3. Betts, Jennifer. "Actionable Long-Term Goal Examples for College Students." Accessed May 14, 2021. https://examples.yourdictionary.com/actionable-long-term-goal-examples-for-college-students.html.

4. Hyatt, Michael. "How Evernote Can Help You Achieve Your Goals." Evernote Blog (blog), December 29, 2014. https://evernote.com/blog/how-evernote-can-help-you-achieve-your-goals/.

5. Crystal. "Mastering MOOCs with Evernote." Personal Knowledge Management for Academia & Librarians, October 20, 2014. http://www.academicpkm.org/2014/10/20/mastering-moocs-evernote/.

6. Ward, David. Evernote for Lawyers: A Guide to Getting Organized & Increasing Productivity. The Attorney Marketing Center, n.d.

7. "19 Practical Evernote Ideas Students Can Begin Using Today." Accessed October 13, 2017. https://evernoteforstudents.files.wordpress.com/2012/09/19-practical-evernote-ideas1.pdf.

8. Doubek, James. "Attention, Students: Put Your Laptops Away." NPR.org, April 17, 2016. https://www.npr.org/2016/04/17/474525392/attention-students-put-your-laptops-away.

9. Adam, "My Tribute to Evernote: A Student's Guide," The Flannelboard (blog), March 24, 2012, http://theflannelboard.blogspot.com/2012/03/my-tribute-to-evernote-students-guide.html.

10. Geher, Glenn. "22 Tips for First-Year College Students." Psychology Today, August 9, 2018. https://www.psychologytoday.com/blog/darwins-subterranean-world/201808/22-tips-first-year-college-students.

11. Frank, Thomas. "42 College Tips I Learned Freshman Year." College Info Geek, March 4, 2011. https://collegeinfogeek.com/42-things-i-learned-freshman-year/.

12. "5 Tips to Use Evernote For Academic Achievement," Evernote Blog, April 14, 2014, http://blog.evernote.com/blog/2014/04/14/5-tips-use-evernote-academic-achievement/.

13. Joy Suzanne Hunt, "How to Use Evernote to Organize Research," The Cafe Scholar (blog), July 24, 2017, https://www.thecafescholar.com/use-evernote-organize-research/.

14. National Society of High School Scholars. "How to Survive Freshman Year of College," July 6, 2018. https://www.nshss.org/blog/how-to-survive-freshman-year-of-college/.

15. Collins, Brandon. 2012. The 2 Hour Guide to Mastering Evernote - Including: Tips, Uses, and Evernote Essentials. 2nd ed. Future Prophet Publishing LLC.

16. Kowalczyk, Piotr. "8 Evernote Tips for Book Lovers." Ebook Friendly (blog), May 15, 2014. http://ebookfriendly.com/evernote-tips-for-booklovers/.

17. Collins, The 2 Hour Guide to Mastering Evernote - Including.

18. Travis Mitchell and Emma Kerr, "12 Ways to Prepare for Your Freshman Year of College," U.S. News & World Report, June 29, 2020, https://www.usnews.com/education/best-colleges/slideshows/10-ways-to-prepare-for-your-freshman-year-of-college.

19. Milligan, Jonathan. "A Simple Guide to Indexing the Books You Read for Evernote." JonathanMilligan.com, June 4, 2014. http://jonathanmilligan.com/a-simple-guide-to-indexing-the-books-you-read-for-evernote/.

20. Collins, The 2 Hour Guide to Mastering Evernote - Including.

21. Michael Hyatt, "A Better Filing System for Public Speakers (and Writers)," Michael Hyatt & Co., February 18, 2011, https://michaelhyatt.com/how-to-use-evernote-if-you-are-a-speaker-or-writer.html.

22. Collins, The 2 Hour Guide to Mastering Evernote - Including.

23. Ibid.

24. "10 Tips for Using Evernote to De-Stress College from Student Ambassador Megan Cotter," Evernote Blog, April 18, 2012, https://blog.evernote.com/blog/2012/04/18/10-tips-for-using-evernote-to-de-stress-college-from-student-ambassador-megan-cotter/.

Chapter Six

Planning Your Day

Congratulations on making it through your first day! You now only have roughly 1,400 more days until you earn your bachelor's degree. You are going to need to develop a routine or system to help you stay on track throughout your degree program. Others will count on you when you create a system you can trust. [1]

In this chapter, we are going to explore ideas for developing a routine that will keep you on target to success. You will learn what goes into a daily as well as a weekly routine. Finally, you will learn about strategies for keeping your notes organized.

Setting Routines

A daily and weekly routine will help you overcome procrastination. Michael Hyatt advocates for developing an ideal week. [2] Plot out what you would like your week to resemble. You can do this on a paper planner, but I am going to suggest Evernote. Hyatt plots his morning and evening routines as well as his workday startup and shutdown routines. The more you can control your schedule, the more time you will get back.

Consider the following when you plot your ideal week:

- Class schedule
- Office hours
- Study time
- Work

- Visiting with friends

- Fitness

- Transit time to class or work

- Fun activities

- Sleeping

- Eating

- Reading

Morning Routine

How does your morning routine look? Many students miss out on meals and fitness because they have not built them into a routine. What do you do during the first 60-90 minutes of the day? A morning routine would be a great time to do some reading and fitness. We are often too tired and just want to relax at the end of the day.

Evening Routine

Closing your day is also an essential routine to stay on track. An evening routine is a good time to review what you will be doing tomorrow and during the next few days. Ensure your titles and tags are set and you placed your notes in the correct notebook. Create links between notes to help get the information you need when you need it. Review your homework planner. What is coming up? Do you have a plan to ensure you get your homework turned in on time, chapters read, and papers written? Nothing will set you back faster than procrastination.

Weekly Routine

You should set aside time in your schedule once a week to review your calendar. Look at least one week in the past to ensure you have not missed anything. It is important to look over your schedule for the next week. This will help you avoid any surprises.

Reviewing your schedule also helps your brain create open loops. You will then be mentally working on the different projects in your subconscious. You will have already contributed mental energy to the project when it comes time to do the actual work on the upcoming project.

It is up to you when you do this, but Sunday evening is a standard prep time.

Strategies to Keep You on Track

Your daily and weekly reviews are a great time to do some Evernote housekeeping. I am going to share some different tactics that will help keep you on track. These tactics focus on task management with Getting Things Done (GTD), organizing and reviewing notes, using reminders, and merging notes.

Getting Things Done

The first strategy I would like to discuss with you originated with David Allen. Allen calls it GTD. The idea of the GTD system is to work on a document for as little time as possible. You must decide what to do with each email, handout, or other materials you receive. These decisions include immediately reacting on it, delegating it to someone else, filing it as a reference document, discarding it, or placing it in a project for you to work on it later.

David Donaldson and Joe Allen, in their book, *Getting Things Done the David Allen Way with Evernote: A Beginner's Guidebook on How to Master GTD with Evernote*, outlined a process for combining the GTD process and Evernote. I use a version of their strategy for maintaining my world in Evernote.

Here are some GTD system notebooks to consider:

Inbox

You should have created this notebook in Chapter Three. This notebook's only purpose is to catch all the incoming documents, messages, and tasks. You should review this notebook often and decide what you want to do with each note. Empty this notebook at the end of each review if possible. Ideally, you should clear out the inbox once a day.

Reference

A reference notebook stores documents for use sometime in the future. These could be user manuals, software codes, or other must-have documents.

Projects

Projects are significant tasks that have many subtasks and a date when they will end. Create a separate notebook for each project and place them in a notebook stack. Place notes with the details of each task within each project notebook. You should have a master note with an outline of all the tasks requiring completion. Your project notebook stack is another set of notebooks that you should review often. Archive a project notebook to get it off your mind when you complete the project.

Delegated Tasks

You may not be responsible for completing all the tasks you receive. Instead, you may want to delegate some tasks to people better suited for accomplishing them. But you will want to keep track of the task to ensure the other person completes it. A **Delegated Tasks** notebook is a great place to put these tasks as a reminder. Review this notebook to check on the status of the assignment on a regular basis. Refile the note once the individual has completed the task.

Another strategy for managing delegated tasks is to tag them with the word "delegated" rather than place them in a separate notebook.[3] You could then set up a search for the word "delegated" to see all these types of notes. You could then remove the tag upon task completion.

Keeping Evernote Organized

Evernote can turn into a real mess if you do not make it a habit to keep it organized. A messy Evernote will defeat the initial purpose of being more organized.

David Ward, author of *Evernote for Lawyers: A Guide to Getting Organized & Increasing Productivity,* shared a strategy for reviewing your Evernote system weekly. Here are his steps:

Scan Loose Documents to Evernote

Scan all loose papers to Evernote weekly and discard them. Scanning new documents should be a daily routine while you are taking classes. These notes will first go to your inbox.

Zero Email

Review your email messages and decide if you need to save the message for future action or reference. Archive the message once you have finished with it.

Review Calendar (Last Week, Next Week)

Review your calendar entries. Add or review notes as necessary. Place a note link in the calendar entry if there is a relationship between the event and note.

Review Your Evernote Notes for Completeness

You will review every note in your inbox in this essential step. You will give it a proper title, add tags, improve it, and finally, assign it to a notebook.

Review Course Notebook

Review your course notebooks and course master notes just to make sure everything is on track.

Review Action Lists (!when)

Assign tags related to when you must complete a task if you are adhering to the GTD method for staying on track. Take time to review your "When" tags (e.g., ~MIT!, ~1-Now, ~51-someday, etc.) to see if you have completed the task. Change the !when tag to ~99-done when you complete the task. Update these tags as the tasks start to take on a higher priority.

Review Projects

These weekly reviews are also an excellent time to review projects just to make sure everything is on track.

Review Waiting Lists

Are you waiting for someone to complete a task for you? If so, these tasks should have a "delegated" tag associated with them so you can find them.

Review Someday Lists

Finally, take time to review the notes with a someday tag to see if they are ready to turn into unique projects.

Look for projects and other notes that have served their purpose and are ready for you to archive them. You can change the notebook for a note when it no longer needs to be on your radar. I have a notebook called "Processed" where I place these types of notes. A bulk of my 8,000 notes are in this notebook. Just ensure they have good titles and tags.

Evernote will turn out to be an incredible organizational system if you take time and discipline yourself to manage it.

Setting Reminders

Reminders are another feature that will make notes more useful to you. You will receive an email in the morning when the reminder is due if you set a time and date for your note. Email reminders will work if you set the option to receive them.

Setting Reminders on Notes

You will see an option for adding a reminder on the lower-left corner of your note. Clicking on the reminder link will provide you with an opportunity to add a date. Select to receive a notification: tomorrow, in two days, in a week, or you can set a date.

The reminder will show up in the reminder list just above the **Notes List**.

Clicking on the note with a reminder in the **Reminder List** will let you see when the reminder is due or past due. You can mark the note as done, clear the reminder, or edit the date of the reminder by clicking on **Reminder**. Evernote will strike out the reminder date and time if you mark it done. Evernote will remove the reminder if you clear the reminder. Finally, Evernote will present you with the same "set the date" options if you want to change the date.

Merging Notes

There are times when you discover you need to combine two or more notes into one. Combining various notes into a single note is quite easy. Select the notes you wish to merge from the notes list. You will have to hold down the **Ctrl** key as you select the different notes. The notes list will show you the notes you have chosen. Additionally, it will show you various options. Merge is one of the options. Selecting the **Merge** button will combine your selected notes into a single note. **WARNING!** There is no feature to undo this action, and there is no warning beforehand. Also, merging is not available on Evernote for iOS, Evernote for Android, or Evernote Web.

Wrap Up

Creating a daily and weekly routine will help you be more successful as a college student. You will be able to stay on track and not let anything slip through the cracks by reviewing your notes and notebooks daily. You will increase your awareness of upcoming assignments by reviewing your notes weekly. These reviews will lead to improved performance. The next chapter will show you how to retrieve notes through the power of search.

***

1. Stachowiak, Bonni Jean. The Productive Online and Offline Professor: A Practical Guide. First edition. Thrive Online Series. Sterling, Virginia: Stylus Publishing, 2020.
2. Hyatt, Michael S. Free to Focus: A Total Productivity System to Achieve More by Doing Less. Grand Rapids, Michigan: Baker Book, a division of Baker Publishing Group, 2019.
3. Donaldson, David, and Joe Allen. Getting Things Done the David Allen Way with Evernote: A Beginner's Guidebook on How to Master GTD with Evernote, n.d.

Chapter Seven

Powerful Search Capability

I have talked throughout this book about using a search to retrieve your notes. One of the fastest ways of finding notes is through Evernote's search. Evernote's search will help find what you need when searching by date, tags, text, or size. You can also search through attachments to include images. Yes, Evernote will also identify text in images.

Ways to Search

There are two primary ways to search for notes in Evernote. You can select a notebook or tag and scan through the notes list or you can use the search box.

Remember when we discussed applying good titles and tags to your notes? This is when it comes in handy. All the information included when you processed your notes will help you find the note when you need it.

Scanning

One of the simplest ways to find your notes is to scan for them. Scanning for notes becomes more challenging as you build out your repository. The scanning method is quite easy. Click on a notebook or tag and then look through the notes list to find the desired note or notes. Change notebooks or tags as appropriate.

Searching

Unless I know the location of a note, the method I use the most is searching. You can search for a word or phrase by entering it in the search box at the top of the notes list. Evernote will begin to narrow the list of notes in the notes list as you start to type in your query. It will show you the matching search query just below the search box. Additionally, Evernote will also inform you if it found notes with similar attributes.

If you only want to search a specific notebook or tag, click the desired notebook or tag prior to conducting a search. Otherwise, you can add the notebook or tag as a filter. Regardless, Evernote will still let you know if other notes are matching your query in other areas of Evernote.

Many factors including the information in your note, how well you write your search query, and where you search affect your ability to locate your notes. These are all factors you can adjust along the way. Let's look at building a search query.

Search Operator

Learning Evernote's search operators is essential. A search operator is a command that narrows the scope of a search to help you find your desired notes. Appendix A has a list of commonly used operators, along with a description of what they do as well as how to use them. You can use multiple operators to help find the exact note you are looking for as you build your search queries. Here are some basic principles:

• Evernote will return a list of notes based on the word or words you place in the search box if you do not use a search operator.

• Evernote will return a list of notes that have ALL the words used in the search query.

• Evernote will only return notes with the exact phrase if the query has the phrase in quotes.

Here are some examples of a search query (bold) and the results.

• **Smith** searches for notes with the term Smith in it.

• **Smith Jones** searches for notes with the terms Smith AND Jones in it.

• **"Smith Jones"** searches for notes with the exact phrasing of Smith Jones.

- Adding an asterisk (*) to the end of a word will return variations of the word. For example, **temp*** would return notes with words such as temporary, temperature, tempo, etc.

Additionally, you can learn more about search query operators by going to Evernote's search grammar page (https://dev.Evernote.com/doc/articles/search_grammar.php).

Using Operators

You can create some precise search queries with these search operators. For example, if you wanted to search your biology notebook for notes created before February 28, 2019, with the tags handout frogs but not tagged with newts you would search for:

notebook:biology created:20190228 tag:handout tag:frogs -tag:newts

Saving Searches

You don't want to rewrite frequently used search queries every time you need it. The best thing to do is save the query if you use it often. I have a list of queries I use again and again to help manage my Evernote.

Save a search query if you have used the same query more than twice. Saved queries will save you time later. The purpose of using Evernote is to help you save time and energy!

You will find your saved search queries listed in the **Saved Searches** tool on the sidebar. You can add your saved query to your shortcut bar for quick access if it is one you use often.

Saving a Search Query

Follow these steps to keep your search query:

1. Enter your search query in the search box and run it. It is a great way to test if it works.

2. Click on the **More Options** button from the Search results list. Finally, click on **Save Search** menu item.

3. Update the name and click the **Save** button.

Saving Search Query to Shortcuts

Adding a saved search query to your shortcuts is rather simple. Right-click on your saved search and select the **Add to Shortcuts** option.

You can rearrange your shortcuts list by clicking on a shortcut and drag it up and down the list.

My Favorite Search Queries

I have created many saved searches over time. Here are my favorites to help you get started.

- **created:day-1** - Notes I have created since yesterday.

- **tag:~MIT!** - Notes tagged as my most important thing (MIT).

- **tag:~1-Now** - Notes following GTD strategy. These are tasks that I want to do today.

- **tag:~2-Next todo:false** - Notes following GTD strategy. These are tasks I have scheduled to do next that have empty checkboxes.

- **-tag:~99-done tag:/Blog** - These are my blog ideas I have not yet written.

- **any: created:day updated:day** - These are notes I need to review during my daily review. This query helps me identify these notes.

- **notebook:Processed -tag:*** - Helps me find notes in my "Processed" notebook without tags.

- **-tag:~99-done tag:/jobsearch** - These are notes I am tracking during job searches that are still open

- **created:month-1 updated:month-1 -tag:*** - This query lets me capture notes that I have not tagged during my monthly review.

- **tag:~51-someday todo:false** - Notes following GTD strategy. These are tasks that I want to do someday.

- **todo:false** - Notes that have an open checkbox.

- **todo:true -todo:false** - Notes listing all completed tasks.

- **intitle:untitled** - These are all the untitled notes.

- **any: created:day-7 updated:day-7** - This search query lets me review notes for the past week.

- **reminderTime:day -reminderTime:day+7** - This search query will return all notes with a reminder for the next seven days.

Preparing for Better Search Results

As you can see, the search feature is mighty. You should have no problem finding your notes. But there are things you can do to help ensure you find the notes when you need them. Here are some guidelines to help you improve your system:

Note Titles/Naming Convention

Ensure you are putting key terms in the title and body of your notes. Make your titles and note bodies as informative as possible. Rewrite the titles of notes if necessary. Rewriting titles is usually applicable when you send an email to Evernote.

Ensure you are consistent with the format if you use names or dates in note titles. I recommend YYYYMMDD for including a date. Use the format Date/Vendor/Amount if you are adding receipts to Evernote. [1]

Creating Strong and Consistent Tags

You need to take steps to ensure consistency when creating tags. Evernote will add a new tag if you create a new variation of a current tag. Decide if a tag is to be singular or plural. You must decide upon one convention, e.g., "assignment" versus "assignments" or "handout" versus "handouts."

Evernote Works Best With One-Word Tags

Either remove the spaces or use underscores, for example, "periodic table" would become "periodictable" or "periodic_table" if you must use multiple words for a tag.

Prune Tags

One of the other things you will want to do is prune your tag list at regular intervals. As you review your tags, you will see that you have not used some tags. You will want to delete these tags. You may also see a conflict between singular and plural tags. Decide which one you want to use, add the tag to all the notes, and remove the tag you do not wish to use.

Use Prefixes

Adding prefixes to some tags to help with sorting is another strategy you might want to consider.[2] For example, the GTD tags related to time all have a hashtag "~": ~MIT!, ~Now, ~someday, etc. Note: the original GTD "when" tags used a hashtag but it interferes with Evernote's email function. I also use a colon ":" to prefix people or organizations such as :CAP, :Skrabut_Stan, etc.

Stack Tags

Finally, you can also stack tags. Stacking tags means you can group them. You can find more information on this in Chapter Three.

Search Images

Evernote can search through images for text that matches your text query through a feature called OCR. Evernote will recognize text in your images, PDFs, and Ink notes. Evernote could also find search queries within your handwritten notes. Success depends on the quality of your handwriting.

I will take pictures of whiteboards, projected slides, posters, signs, etc. because of this capability. I can then later find the note by searching.

Wrap Up

Evernote has a powerful search capability that will help you find your notes in a flash. Take time to experiment with it and set up saved searches. You will increase your level of productivity with strategic saved searches. You will find that you will be using search quite a bit as you continue to save information to Evernote. In the next chapter, you are going to learn how to use Evernote to prepare for quizzes and exams as well as complete assignments.

***

1. Ward, David. Evernote for Lawyers: A Guide to Getting Organized &
Increasing Productivity. The Attorney Marketing Center, n.d.
2. Ibid.

Chapter Eight

Managing Course Assignments

Let's discuss strategies for using Evernote to complete various homework assignments now that you have a better idea of how to use the program to stay on track. These strategies may include preparing for an exam, completing lab notebooks, writing papers, researching for papers or presentations, and participating in group assignments.

Evernote can help you handle these different assignments. Getting the greatest benefit is a matter of self-discipline in your Evernote use.

Preparing for a Quiz or Exam

Having all your notes on hand is one of the benefits of saving all your notes to Evernote. You can open Evernote to review class notes whenever you have a free moment. You should do this often. Research has shown daily reviews yield better results than an all-night cram session.

There are many advantages of digitized notes. For example, you can search through your digitized notes quicker than searching through a stack of paper notes. [1] Enhance your ability to find your notes by adding tags and clear titles.

Here are some tips for developing an effective study strategy:

• "Look over your notes from the last class before class and then review your notes right after class." [2]

• Find a specific place to study. It should be different than where you do other things such as sleep, eat, or play games. You want to condition yourself to study in a designated place.

- Make flashcards or create your own quizzes.[3] It is an active studying method.

- Block out time on your calendar to study.[4]

- Identify critical events such as exams and quizzes on your calendar. Block out extra time on your calendar dedicated to preparing for these activities.[5]

There are many different ways to prepare for quizzes and exams. I prefer active study strategies such as flashcards, practice exams, and the SQ3R method. I described the SQ3R method in Chapter Five. It is time to look at flashcards and practice exams.

Creating Flashcards

Instructors will encourage you to create study aids such as flashcards to help prepare for exams. Flashcards are an active learning strategy and a great way to prepare. I have some excellent news for you! Some applications work together with Evernote to create great flashcards and other quizzing tools. Here are some examples:

- Reflect - https://www.reflectapp.io/

- Eidetic - http://www.eideticapp.com/

Each program has a unique way to add content into Evernote so you will have a front and back version of the "card." Often, the title is the "question," and the body of the Evernote message is the "answer." Adding new cards is effortless once you know the format. Some of the flashcard programs will also let you add audio clips and images. You should add new cards throughout your term. You can use SQ3R strategies to help design study questions (See Chapter Five).

Flashcards are useful for learning new vocabulary, foreign languages, mathematical formulas, and so much more.[6] Using flashcards is powerful because you can control what is on the card and how it is displayed. The different programs I shared here can also turn studying into a game in which the application keeps score. You can also create different study flashcard decks.

Tips for Flashcard Success

There are many different options for building a flashcard set. You could:

• Create a notebook for each flashcard set and add your questions as separate notes.

• Create a notebook for a topic such as geography and add all your flashcards as separate notes. The difference is you would use a tag to identify different flashcard sets.

• Moving cards from one notebook to another allows you to build unique study flashcard sets.

Building Practice Exams

Practice exams are another effective way to prepare for a major exam. They take time to create, but these are useful tools to help prepare for your midterm and final exams. Create an exam with a separate answer sheet in Evernote. You could share them with the rest of your study group. Likewise, you could add exams to the set your study group has prepared.

Your exam development should begin with the course objectives the instructor shared. Course objectives are the main points your instructor wants you to know by the end of the course. These form the basis of great practice questions. Next, review the notes you took in class. Your instructor shared this content with you for a reason. Jot down questions as you are doing your daily review of your notes. Additionally, note things that will make a good exam question as you are reading your textbook.[7] These strategies will make studying easier as you prepare your practice exam.

You can also ask your instructors for previous exams they gave for prior classes. Work with your classmates to build a larger test bank from which you can draw questions.

Lab Notebooks

Many classes in college have hands-on activities. You will have a lab for some of these classes. The labs may be for chemistry, biology, or one of the other sciences. You will also have to do labs or work in a lab environment for classes like engineering, physics, and computer science. Evernote is an excellent tool for creating a lab notebook. One of the most significant benefits is you do not have to carry a bulky notebook around. You will never lose your notes.

Naturally, you should create a notebook where you can place your lab notes. Place this notebook with your class notebook. Create a template as a starter note if your instructor has a specific format for your lab reports. You would then copy the template as a new note. Key components of your template should include researchers' names, experimental objectives, materials, procedure (with observations), data, and conclusions. [8]

You can digitize instructor handouts and link to them from your lab note. You can also either link to or embed other content to your note, such as spreadsheets, images, or lab results.

Ideally, you will have access to a computer or a mobile device such as an iPad or tablet while conducting your lab experiments. You can then immediately be working on your final report as you do your lab work. The great thing about using Evernote while you are working is you can quickly access your results from your personal computer when back in your room or the library.

You can cut and paste or type in essential coding functions for your computer science classes. Additionally, you can take pictures of wiring diagrams or flowcharts and save them to Evernote.

You can either create a drawing on paper and digitize it or use one of the many digital drawing programs that work with Evernote to create sketches to support your lab notes. Penultimate and Sketchbook are a couple of the programs I use. I also use Skitch to annotate an image or PDF file with arrows, text, and shapes.

Add audio clips to your lab notes to add clarity as well as remind yourself what you did during the experiment.

Use Evernote on your mobile devices while doing fieldwork research. You can save the results to Evernote.

Submit your final report to your instructor as a shareable link. You can also export the note to upload to your learning management system when you finish collecting your data and writing your report.

Using Evernote will give you a feel for collecting digital data even though Evernote may differ from the tools you may use in the "real world."

Collecting data is a skill that will benefit you in many career fields such as healthcare, medical, research, and computer programming.[9]

Projects

You will receive projects to complete throughout your academic and working life. These projects may be something you work on alone, while other projects need a team effort. Create a separate project notebook stack with a unique notebook for each project. Share a specific notebook with the rest of the team if working collaboratively.

Project Master Note

A project master note is one of the first documents you will want to add to your notebooks. This master note should include a full description of the project with all the known parameters. Create a unique title and add tags to help find the project later.

Your project will often need the completion of tasks and subtasks. List these tasks in your master note. Make the tasks more actionable by adding checkboxes to each of the significant tasks. These tasks will appear when you search for unchecked action items. You can list subtasks on the master note. You can also create a separate note for each major task along with its subtasks. Make these actionable items by adding to-do checkboxes. You can link to the task notes from the master project note.

Save any details you have about the project to the project notebook. These items can be documents, email messages, clarification notes, etc.

Place the project notebook into an archive notebook stack when you finish the project. Archiving the folder will remove it from your things-to-do list.

Conducting Research

You are going to do a lot of research for papers and projects while in college. You need to create a system to help you gather, organize, and make sense of what you discover. this is an excellent opportunity to tie back all the reasons they should keep track of their research, quotes, ideas of others, facts and figures in Evernote so it is easily referenced when the student writes a paper so they can properly cite the author and include appropriate bibliographic references.

Use Evernote for all your research and writing projects. It is a useful place to capture and keep track of ideas, references, and files related to your project. You can then reference this material so that you can cite the author and include appropriate bibliographic references. You will find Evernote a powerful tool as you investigate your dissertation or thesis topic. Evernote was one of my primary tools as I was preparing to write this book. I saved the research material to Evernote as I scoured the internet.

You can capitalize on digital resources. A significant number of academic journals are in PDF or HTML format. You can find digitized books on Google Books or Project Gutenberg. Digitized content will make researching a lot easier. [10]

Here are some things I learned:

Create a Notebook for Collecting Your Research

Create a notebook for collecting your research. Each of your projects should have a notebook. Share group project notebooks with your group members. Place your research notebook with your course notebook.

Put all your research into these notebooks. Your research can be PDF articles, clipped web pages, typed notes, images, audio notes, etc.

Add meaningful tags and titles to your notes so you can access your research on a specific subject easier.

Ensure you capture all the bibliographic information about the content. A simple way to do this for a book is by taking a picture of the book's reference page.

Capture Everything Related to Your Research

Every time you see something that relates to your research topic, capture it. You will have everything at your fingertips when it comes time to write your paper. You can then focus on crafting your paper.

Create a Separate Note for Each Piece of Research

Each piece of research should be a different note. Break each note into its smallest part. Unique titles and tags allow you to isolate each topic easier. Taking a picture of a page or pages is an easy way to capture a quote from a book or other document. You can mark up the quote image with Skitch as well as type in supporting notes. [11]

Capture From the Web

There are websites you want to remember as you search the web. You could save the link to your web browser's bookmark section. Unfortunately, you can only store so many links before your browser bogs down. Accessing these links or web pages from all your devices, including public computers, is challenging.

Evernote is a great tool to help you save sites you want to review again and again. It is also a great place to store the contents of a page in case someone changes or deletes the page.

The Evernote Web Clipper is a tool I use all the time to save web pages. The Web Clipper is an extension or add-on for your web browser. It allows you to clip full webpages or even just part of a webpage. You can add notes, tags, and place it in a notebook once you have clipped a webpage.

Clipping a webpage to your Evernote collection is as easy as a simple click on the Web Clipper. You have an option to save the entire page, a part of the page, a simplified article, a bookmark to the page, or a screenshot of the page.

A link back to the website is available in the note's info section accessible from the Note menu.

You can then markup screenshots of a webpage with the Skitch tools. Markup is a useful capability if you need to explain something to someone or if you just want to take some notes.

Another way to save a page URL is to drag the URL from the browser's address bar to Evernote. [12] Dragging a URL will work for the desktop client. You can drag the URL into an open note if you are using the web program.

You can use Web Clipper's "simplified article" feature to strip distracting advertisements from articles you wish to save. Removing distracting material will let you focus on your content.

Clipping Pages with Web Clipper

Click on the **Web Clipper** button when you find an article you want to save. Evernote will provide you with five options:

- **Article** - This version will focus on the main section of the page and ignore the rest.

- **Simplified article** - This version strips formatting and layouts to just focus on the content.

- **Full page** - Clips a static copy of the entire page.

- **Bookmark** - This option clips the URL along with a short snippet of text and a thumbnail of the page.

- **Screenshot** - The screenshot version allows you to select a part of the screen to clip. You can then make annotations and highlight other vital parts of the image.

You can make the following updates before saving with the Web Clipper:

- Update Title

- Assign a notebook

- Add one or more tags

- Add remarks or more comments.

Clipping Pages with a Mobile Device

You can also clip pages you find while using your mobile device. Click on the share button for your mobile browser when you find a page that you want to save. Select the **Save to Evernote** option.

Evernote will save the full page to Evernote with Android applications. You have an option to select the notebook and tags you want to use with iOS devices.

Strategies for Using the Web Clipper

The Web Clipper allows you to clip entire web-based articles or just parts of the page. Here are some ideas for information you should consider collecting with Evernote:

- Articles about a specific topic or line of research. You can enhance these articles with your notes, images, and audio files.

- Quotes for presentations or to support papers you write. You can build your library of inspirational and informative quotes.

- Save your library research search results when searching through digital collections. It can be quite easy to get lost when doing research. It is easy to lose track of a great article you just saw.

- "When using Google Scholar or Google Books, capture a screenshot with the Web Clipper rather than the full page. Ensure you are also capturing the citation information."[13]

Capture Audio Notes

Don't forget you can capture audio notes when collecting research. You can support audio notes with images, text, and other content.

Capture the Geolocation of Where a Note was Taken

Turn on the geolocation services for Evernote if the location where you take notes is essential. Geolocation can be important for some research projects, such as the study of wildlife.[14]

Capture Pictures of Your Ideas

Ensure you take a picture of the research ideas you drew on a whiteboard or the post-it notes you used to create a concept map. Save these images to your research notebook.[15]

Sync Your Notes

Take time to sync your notes to the Evernote cloud so your notes are available on all your devices. Syncing your notes is especially important if you have been working offline while doing research or fieldwork.

Archive Notes Into Master Research Notebooks

One of the most powerful things about using Evernote to collect your research is you will have your research notes forever. You can reorganize all your research into a master research notebook once you finish the term or project. Another option is placing your research project notebook into a research notebook stack. A master research notebook will help you with future research projects.

Automating Note Collection

Automation is another method for note collection I would like to touch upon. A trigger causes an action when an event occurs that will send a note to Evernote. One of the tools I use to do this is IFTTT (If This Then That). Another set of tools that I use are Readwise and Hypothes.is. I introduced Readwise earlier. First, let's take a closer look at IFTTT.

Collecting Notes With IFTTT

IFTTT is a web-based service that connects two different programs. For example, it will connect Twitter to Facebook, Evernote, or even your Phillips Hue lights. Connecting programs allows you to automate processes you would spend a lot of time doing by hand. For example, you could collect favorite Tweets into Evernote without having to copy and paste them yourself.

How IFTTT Works. IFTTT uses applets. An applet has three pieces: a channel that outputs information, a trigger, and a channel action that inputs information. Here is an example using Twitter and Evernote. Something happens with the first channel (Twitter), such as I favor a Tweet. Favoring the Tweet would be my trigger and cause the next action, in this case, Evernote records the Tweet (2nd Channel).

IFTTT has many different channels you can use. These channels include social media programs, productivity, news, blogging, business, connected home, commerce, fitness, wearables, lifestyle, mobile, music, photos, etc.

Creating an IFTTT Applet. Create an account on IFTTT and then register the channels you want to use. IFTTT will ask you to connect with your login information for channels you wish to use. In this example, I am going to save my favorite Tweets to Evernote. Let me show you the process.

1. Click on the **Create** button from the menu bar from the IFTTT home page.

2. Click on the word "Add" for the If This step.

3. Search for Twitter and select it.

4. Choose a trigger. In this example, I will be choosing "New liked tweet by you." You may have to provide extra information called ingredients.

5. Now, select the word "Add" for the Then That step.

6. Search for Evernote and select it.

7. Choose an action. In this case, I will "Create a note."

8. Update the ingredients and select the **Create Action** button.

9. Click on **Continue**.

10. Update the applet title and select the **Finish** button.

11. Congratulations! You have created an IFTTT applet.

Applet Recommendations. You can find applets you can adapt if you look through the different channels. Adapting applets is a quick way to put together a collection as well as generate ideas for applet combinations.

You will find over 1,000 applets if you search for Evernote using the search bar at the top of the IFTTT page. Think about combinations that would benefit the learning platform you are building. Here are some applets I recommend:

- Make an Evernote journal based on your Google Calendar.
- Save your archived lists in Pocket to Evernote.
- Save starred Gmail messages to Evernote.
- Speak notes to Evernote using Siri and iOS Reminders.
- Save your Favorite tweets to Evernote.
- Create link notes in Evernote from Feedly articles saved for later.
- Keep a list of new bestseller books for Kindle.
- Add your "Watch Later" videos to Evernote.
- Save blog posts or other RSS feed items to Evernote.
- Archive your Facebook posts to Evernote.
- Save Facebook, Twitter, Instagram, or Flickr pictures to Evernote.

• Use Evernote to log your social media activity as a 24/7 journal.

This list of applets should provide some ideas of what you could capture using IFTTT and Evernote. You can put capturing everyday tasks on autopilot so you will not miss anything. You can then focus on your studies.

Collecting Notes With Readwise and Hypothes.is

I started using Readwise as an easy way to export my Kindle notes and highlights into Evernote. Kindle is not the only application you can connect Readwise to. Readwise will sync with 12 different applications such as Twitter, Hypothes.is, Goodreads, Feedly, Instapaper, Pocket, and many more. I have also connected to Hypothes.is.

Hypothes.is. Hypothes.is is a social annotation tool that you can use to make annotations to a webpage or PDF document. You can make public or private notes as an individual, in groups, or as part of the general public.

Your notes become more useful if you can retrieve them from Hypothes.is. You can send all the notes you take to Evernote once you configure Readwise to capture Hypothes.is notes.

Readwise will create a unique document in Evernote for each document that you review. All Readwise notes go to a Readwise notebook in Evernote. My research efforts are much easier and faster since I started to take notes with Hypothes.is and Readwise. I open up Evernote when it is time to start writing because all my notes are there.

Keeping Track of Information

In addition to tracking the significant items related to classes, you can use Evernote to track many smaller, but useful, items. Here are some examples.

Quotes

Capture inspirational quotes related to your interests. You can type it in, add a meme, take a picture, or capture an audio note. These quotes are useful for presentations, papers, and social media. You may want to create a separate notebook just for quotes.

Current Events

Some classes have you track current events. I recommend creating a separate notebook for current events. Adding related articles to the notebook is easy with the Web Clipper or collecting articles with an IFTTT applet. [16] You will then have these events on hand when needed.

Glossary/Dictionary

You are going to come across words you don't know while reading. Creating a vocabulary list or glossary is one recommended tactic for learning those words. Create an Evernote note to write in all the new words you discover along with their definitions. Review this list often to become familiar with the terms. You can also add audio clips with the pronunciations. Add images if they are essential to learning the new word.

Computer Code

Evernote is a convenient place to store code snippets if you code. You can title them with a meaningful name as well as add tags to clarify the language used and function. There are certain pieces of code I use over and over. Storing them in Evernote helps speed up the coding process.

Music Details

There are many things you can include in a music notebook. Most importantly, you can upload PDFs or images of your sheet music. Mark up the documents to add a better understanding. Include audio clips of the music to have as a ready resource. You can also upload the program announcements and guides when you have a performance.

Another notebook and list I have created are for my favorite sheet music and tablature. I will scan in my favorite music and tabs as notes, or I will upload a PDF file. I have these different notes linked to a master music list. I have a convenient music library at my fingertips. It is easy to scroll through the music as you are playing it. You can also resize it to reduce the amount of scrolling.

Writing Your Paper

You can not only research your paper with Evernote but also draft your document. Evernote has all the tools needed to format your draft. Here are some strategies to consider when developing your paper.

Create a Notebook for Your Writing Project

Create a notebook for your writing project. Your writing project notebook is separate from your research notebook.

Create a Master Table of Contents Note

Create a master table of contents note where you will link all the subparts.

Create a Reference Note

Create a reference note where you will store all the references as you add content to your paper. You will be able to link them to your research content.

Title Your Subparts

Use prefixes to show different phases of your document parts. For example, use a "!" - title when you complete a part.

Create an Outline Note

An outline note is one of the first notes you will want to create. You can skim through research resources to develop your outline. You can start writing about each of your points once you have an outline. Use a separate note for each major point. Ensure you give them a meaningful title. Save the link to your note on your table of contents once you finish drafting out a section of your paper.

Merge Parts Into First Draft

Merge all the subparts into your first draft when you have all the pieces written. Ensure you title it appropriately. Take a moment to reorganize the sections as needed. Make a copy of this note and give it a title that will show it is a second draft. Use this draft to make your edits. Keep repeating this process until you get to your final draft. Ensure you are updating your references and table of contents while working on the draft.

Create a Final Draft

Copy the contents to the word processor you plan to use when you have gotten to your final draft. You can then finish the layout for submission.

Track Your Writing Process

You can also use Evernote to track your writing progress. Build out a writing schedule to ensure you are on track to finish your paper on time. You can and should keep a writing log. A writing log tracks the day and word count.

Store Drafts in the Cloud

One of the great things about using Evernote for your drafts is Evernote stores them in the cloud. You can work on them from any device anywhere.

Group Assignments

You can increase the success of your project by using Evernote as a central research hub. The first place to start is to create a notebook where everyone can share their notes as well as edit the notes of others.

Share project timelines, responsibility matrices, research notes, swipe files, document or presentation drafts, etc. Everyone should be able to contribute to the folder to include making notes in shared documents.

Wrap Up

Evernote is a powerful tool for not only capturing class notes but also building study aids. You will find Evernote useful for collecting research, keeping lab notebooks, and writing papers alone or with others. In the next chapter, we are going to look at how to use Evernote for other essential activities related to college and the time beyond college.

***

1. Walsh, Emily, and Ilseung Cho. "Using Evernote as an Electronic Lab Notebook in a Translational Science Laboratory." Journal of Laboratory Automation 18, no. 3 (June 1, 2013): 229–34. https://doi.org/10.1177/2211068212471834.

2. National Society of High School Scholars. "How to Survive Freshman Year of College," July 6, 2018. https://www.nshss.org/blog/how-to-survive-freshman-year-of-college/.

3. Frank, Thomas. "42 College Tips I Learned Freshman Year." College Info Geek, March 4, 2011. https://collegeinfogeek.com/42-things-i-learned-freshman-year/.

4. "How to Survive Freshman Year of College."

5. Ibid.

6. Alhinty, Mona. "English-Language Learning at Their Fingertips." International Journal of Mobile and Blended Learning 7, no. 2 (January 1, 2015): 45–63. https://doi.org/10.4018/ijmbl.2015040104.

7. Peterson, Deb. "Why You Should Write Practice Tests While You Study." ThoughtCo, May 30, 2019. https://www.thoughtco.com/make-practice-tests-while-you-study-31622.

8. Van Dyke, Aaron R., and Jillian Smith-Carpenter. "Bring Your Own Device: A Digital Notebook for Undergraduate Biochemistry Laboratory Using a Free, Cross-Platform Application." Journal of Chemical Education 94, no. 5 (May 1, 2017): 656.

9. Ibid.

10. "Using Evernote for Research," Indiana Jen, February 28, 2013, https://indianajen.com/2013/02/28/using-evernote-for-research/.

11. Kowalczyk, Piotr. "8 Evernote Tips for Book Lovers." Ebook Friendly (blog), May 15, 2014. http://ebookfriendly.com/evernote-tips-for-booklovers/.

12. Collins, Brandon. 2012. The 2 Hour Guide to Mastering Evernote - Including: Tips, Uses, and Evernote Essentials. 2nd ed. Future Prophet Publishing LLC.

13. Joy Suzanne Hunt, "How to Use Evernote to Organize Research," The Cafe Scholar (blog), July 24, 2017, https://www.thecafescholar.com/use-evernote-organize-research/.

14. Price, S., C. Jewitt, and M. Sakr. "Embodied Experiences of Place: A Study of History Learning with Mobile Technologies." Journal of Computer Assisted Learning 32, no. 4 (August 1, 2016): 345. https://doi.org/10.1111/jcal.12137.

15. DeSchryver, Michael. "Web-Mediated Knowledge Synthesis for Educators." Journal of Adolescent & Adult Literacy 58, no. 5 (February 1, 2015): 388–96. https://doi.org/10.1002/jaal.373.

16. Melissa Seideman, "Part 2: Evernote for the Social Studies | Not Another History Teacher," accessed October 13, 2017, http://notanotherhistoryteacher.edublogs.org/2012/09/14/part-2-evernote-for-the-social-studies/.

Chapter Nine

Your Future with Evernote

There is more to life than studying and going to class. You should become involved in other activities such as sports, student government, theater, etc. to capitalize on the college experience. Perhaps you are working or taking advantage of internships. Travel could have you occupied, whether for conferences or study abroad programs. Evernote can help you be more successful regardless of the activity. Let's take a moment to look at these different activities.

Extracurricular Activities

Colleges sponsor extracurricular activities like volunteer organizations, student organizations, sports, or other activities. These serve as training grounds for learning leadership, team dynamics, organization, and management. Participating in these activities, especially in leadership positions, will provide valuable experience that will give you a leg up in life.[1] You should join something the first day you set foot on campus. "If you have to choose between a double major and getting involved on campus, get involved. All the knowledge in the world won't help you if you come out of college with no experience or professional relationships."[2] Evernote will help you become more successful with these different activities.

Create a separate notebook for each organization or program in which you are a member. You can then place and find notes related to these activities with ease. Store meeting information, research, schedules, etc., in this notebook. This notebook will help you be a more productive participant.

Ensure to apply all the skills and techniques you have learned so far, such as tagging, titling, creating master notes, checklists, etc. The goal is to stay on track and meet your obligations. Nothing is more frustrating to other team members than someone unaware of what is happening and who fails to meet their commitments.

Conferences and Meetings

I don't know if you noticed, but many of the skills you are picking up in college will transfer to the working world. Likewise, the skills you pick up in the working world will help you with college. You will be attending meetings and going to conferences or workshops both in and out of college. Let me share ways Evernote can help you make these experiences more productive.

Travel Info

Evernote is an excellent tool for bringing all your travel information into one place. This information includes flight information, hotel reservations, car rental information, trip itinerary, conference programs, receipts, etc.

Create a notebook stack for all your conferences. Make a separate notebook for each conference. Forward the email you receive for your flights, hotel, and car reservations to Evernote. Place these notes into your conference notebook. I have been doing this for many years. It has made my life so much easier. These documents are at my fingertips when I am traveling. I also have the receipts for my finances.

You can also put together a packing checklist in Evernote. This checklist will help ensure you do not forget anything. Update your list to reflect your lessons learned when you complete your trip. You can then reuse the checklist for your next trip.

Conference Notes

You will have an opportunity to learn many things when attending a conference. Treat the breakout sessions like you would a class. Create a separate note for each session you attend. You can take notes in a variety of ways. Type your notes or use a program like Penultimate to handwrite your notes. You can also add images and audio files to your notes. Likewise, you can attach digitized handouts.

Ensure you take the time to give your notes adequate titles. Additionally, include tags so you can find the notes later. Create a unique tag such as smmw2021. Use this tag for everything related to that conference.

Do you use a paper notebook to collect your notes? If so, snap a picture of the pages and add them to your notebook.

Provide links to your shared notes when sharing your insights from the conference."[3] I include links to my raw notes in the trip reports I write.

Business Cards

Sharing business cards is popular at conferences and workshops. You may find yourself trading business cards with other participants and presenters. Use Evernote's camera feature to take pictures of the business cards. Create a master contact note for your new contacts every evening. As a reminder, business cards are searchable in Evernote. Follow up with new contacts soon after the conference is complete. It is nice to include details of how you met and why you are connecting. You should be able to find these details in your Evernote contact note.

Poster Sessions, Handouts, and Agendas

You can become overloaded with all the handouts, programs, and agendas you pick up at a conference. Take a picture of them as a document and add them to your conference notebook rather than carry them around. The same applies to poster sessions. Take a picture of a poster you find useful.

Trip Reports

I will reflect on my experience and draft a trip report when I finish the conference. The trip report includes information about the conference, a list of the sessions I attended, and key takeaways and action items. I will link back to my raw notes saved in Evernote for each of the sessions. I write my trip report in a word processor such as MS Word or Google Docs and keep a copy in Evernote. Saving a trip report in Evernote makes it easy to share with others. Trip reports are great tools to put ideas into action.

Meeting Agendas and Minutes

You will attend a lot of meetings in your lifetime. Evernote is an excellent tool for collecting all the meeting agendas, minutes, and action items. Create a meeting notebook stack with a separate notebook for each of your committees. Add the meeting agenda to the notebook.

Create and use a meeting agenda template as an efficient way to create your meeting agendas. Share your meeting agenda with others so they can add to it. Here are some items to consider putting in your meeting agenda template:

- **Meeting details**. Date, time, location, virtual connection information.

- **Attendees**. List who should be at the meeting.

- **Meeting goal**. Purpose of the meeting.

- **Meeting topics**. List topics for discussion that lead to the meeting goal.

- **Action items**. Reserve place on your agenda to list action items.

Attach relevant email messages and other documents as you build your schedule.

Typing notes onto the agenda will let you convert it into meeting minutes. You can do this while conducting the meeting. Place action items in the appropriate section of the agenda. Add a checkbox to your action item to identify it. You can create a search query to identify open checkboxes or to-do items throughout your notes. Finding open items will help you ensure that you do not miss anything.

Link to previous meeting notes if your meeting references them.

Ensure you add tags and proper titles to help find and organize your meeting notes.

Study Abroad Trip/Vacation

You can use Evernote to plan for your much-needed vacation or trip just as you would prepare for a conference. Create a separate notebook for your trip. Place your master itinerary in this notebook. Link to your notes for your flight, car, and hotel information in this itinerary. You could also save various destinations you want to explore. Consider sharing your itinerary with family, so they know where to find you in the case of an emergency.

Internship/Work

Evernote is also a powerful tool to use at work or during an internship. You can use Evernote to keep track of resources, people, and knowledge depending upon your role. Here are some typical use cases for Evernote while at work or on an internship.

Human Resource Documents

You will want to keep track of all the documents you get from human resources (HR). These are often the rules and regulations from the company as well as benefits information. Human resources tend to share many printed and digital documents. Digitize all documents and put them in their notebook for quick access. Forward a copy to Evernote to have on hand whenever HR updates their processes, benefits, or schedules. Just give them proper titles and tags.

Process Instructions

Evernote can be a quick access location for essential process instructions. These can be instructions you need to refer to often or just once a year. Set up a notebook stack or notebook for these instructions.

Professional Development

You discovered from creating notes for your classes that Evernote is a powerful learning tool. You are responsible for your continual learning when you leave college. It is professional development. This may take the form of conferences, self-study, reading, online courses, etc. Collect your notes, ideas, and resources into a notebook you can reference anytime. Using Evernote will help you find your notes on topics you have captured. You will improve your knowledge and skills with these lifelong learning strategies.

Annual/Quarterly Planning

Teams often document annual plans on laminated planning calendars or digital calendars.[4] Take a picture of the planning calendar and store it in Evernote for reference.

Do you use a digital calendar for planning? Export the agenda list of the digital calendar and import it into Evernote.

Frequently Asked Questions

You will often be answering questions while interacting with clients, vendors, colleagues, and others. Create a notebook to collect these questions and your answers. This notebook will help you respond to similar issues.

Personnel Management

You will start to be responsible for others as a supervisor sometime during your working career. You will need to keep track of personnel issues in a secure format. Evernote can be an excellent tool for this. Create a personnel notebook stack and notebooks for those whom you supervise. This strategy is like what you would do with contacts. Here are some more notes you may want to consider keeping on your direct report or supervisee.

- **Tracking absences**. Place a time-stamped entry into your master note including the reason for absence and dates.[5]

- **Disciplinary issues**. Include a time-stamped note in your master note anytime you have a conversation with your direct report. Provide enough details to jog your memory later.[6]

- **Exemplary Performance**. Disciplinary issues are not the only thing to log. You also will want to record when your direct report is excelling.

You will want to keep a detailed written record of the successes and challenges of those who report to you. Accurate records will help you if there are issues or when you want to recognize them for superior performance.

Forward emails or other documents related to any of these individuals to Evernote. Place them in the direct report's notebook as well as attach them to the note.

Professional Reading

You are going to do a lot of reading in college. You should continue this habit throughout the rest of your life. As I note in my book *Read to Succeed*, reading is a powerful way to learn new knowledge and pick up new skills. You should squeeze the essence out of the books you read. Taking notes on the books you read is a strategy for doing this is. Some people keep a master note on all the wisdom they glean from books. Others keep a separate note for each book they read. I prefer the latter. I write a blog post on each book and capture the post as a note in Evernote.

Earlier, I shared strategies for capturing notes from the books you read for class. I would like to supplement those strategies with more tactics to use for professional reading. Many variables come into play for what many would consider a simple task. There are different ways to capture your notes, such as making annotations in the book or typing your notes right into Evernote. Each has a slight variation to what you do.

Marking Up Your Book

Use a blank page at the beginning of the book to create an index page to capture the essence of the book if you mark up your book. Capture main points, memorable quotes, and other key points on this index page. Don't forget to include the page number. Take a picture of this page and save it to Evernote once you finish adding notes. Additionally, you could take photos of other essential pieces of the book and save them to Evernote. Add a descriptive title, such as author and page number(s) when you add the pictures.

Adding Notes Into Evernote

You can type your notes to Evernote as you find them or once you get to the end of a chapter. Take a picture of large sections of text and save it to Evernote. Ensure you add a descriptive title for the image, such as the author as well as the page number(s).

Capturing Notes to a Bullet Journal or Commonplace Book

A bullet journal is one of the places where I keep my notes. I will take a picture of the pages relating to a specific book. Always take time to provide a descriptive title.

Master Book Note

You should create a master book note for each of your books. Each master book note should have a picture of the cover and the citation page. Include the author, title, place of publication, and publisher in the title of your note. Merge in all the other notes you created about the book into your master book note. Keep in mind the order you merge the notes. Merge them in the reverse order you saved them. You can then add clarifying notes as appropriate. Add tags to help you locate the book.

Newspaper/Blog/Journal Articles

I usually curate blog posts and other articles to Diigo for future use. At times, I need to have a full article or blog post on hand, such as when I am doing research or traveling. I may save a bunch of articles on Evernote for reading on a plane. It is vital to ensure you sync your reading device before traveling so you have the items ready to read when you lose internet connection. The Web Clipper is invaluable for clipping articles to Evernote.

Writing a Book

You may not consider writing a book right now, but it is something you should consider. It is easier than you think. It is also more possible than ever with self-publishing. I used Evernote to collect all my research material when I started to write this book. Evernote can be a fantastic tool to begin your book projects. One of the prime benefits is it is always available. It means you can work on the book whenever you want.

You can use Evernote from the idea stage to the final draft. Here are some ideas to consider when using Evernote to write your book.

• Build a notebook stack to hold the various parts and phases of your book. Create notebooks for your research, quotes, ideas, character sketches, scene descriptions, etc. What you collect will depend if it is fiction or nonfiction.

• Create notebooks for each phase of your draft, e.g., rough draft, first edit, final edit, etc.

• Write your chapter or chapter sections within each draft notebook.

• Ensure you provide appropriate titles and tags to help identify each section and chapter. Keep in mind Evernote will alphabetize your notes as you are looking at the notebook.

• Use tags to help you relate web pages, articles, photos, etc. to the different chapters you are writing. Try to keep your book structure in mind while you are collecting and tagging information. Ensure you capture the bibliography information for citing as needed.

• Develop an outline master note to help structure your book. You can link various completed sections to this master book note. This will help provide a clue on where you are with writing the book.

• Remove the tags and move a piece of research to another storage notebook if you are not going to use it. I have a notebook called Leftovers.

• Finish your writing in a word processor once you complete your book's draft.

Graduation and Life Beyond

It is time to pivot your use of Evernote as you open up a new chapter in life. Evernote can serve as a digital notebook for all those important events you will be pursuing. It can also serve as a repository of key documents. You already started to collect some of these essential documents.

Here are some things you should be focusing on as you graduate from college.

Job Hunting

Finding a full-time job will be an essential first step as you graduate. You may need to pay off student loans. Evernote has been a crucial tool for me during my job hunting cycles. Keep a boilerplate cover letter and resumé in a job search notebook for quick access. Clip job announcements for positions that interest you using the Web Clipper to your job search notebook.

Additionally, you should create a job-hunting swipe file and store it in Evernote. A job-hunting swipe file is a list of common job application questions with your answers. It makes filling out an application a lot quicker. Update this note as you discover new application questions.

Update Your Contacts Notebook

Ensure you take time to collect contact information for the friends you made in college. Additionally, get contact information for professors with whom you want to maintain a connection. Build out your contacts notebook. Graduation is also an excellent time to reach out to others in your contact folder and let them know you have graduated.

Arrange Your Finances

Forward your receipts to Evernote on a regular basis if you have not already done so. Set up a filter in your email program to send all receipts to Evernote.

Plan Your Move to a New Job

It is time to pull out the moving checklist that you prepared for moving to college. This is a good time to update your moving checklist even if you are waiting to hear back on a job offer. You can build out a detailed moving checklist ready to dust off once you are ready to move. Getting ready to move is a good time to inventory your household items. Evernote is well suited for both tasks.

Set Lifetime Goals

This is a great time to set some life goals. What do you hope to achieve at the end of your lifetime? At the end of ten years? At the end of next year? These goals can be scholarship, personal, work, family, etc. You can then use Evernote as a way to track your progress toward these goals.

Wrap Up

Evernote has served me well for more than a decade. I have used it to look for jobs. It has helped me through two massive multi-state moves. I have also used it to capture ideas for multiple books. I am confident it will also serve you as you shift from academic pursuits to lifelong endeavors. As you can see, Evernote has the flexibility to help you stay on schedule for your classes. It can also help you stay on track for other activities in and out of school. Evernote can help you keep track of it if you can imagine it.

***

1. Geher, Glenn. "22 Tips for First-Year College Students." Psychology Today, August 9, 2018. https://www.psychologytoday.com/blog/darwins-subterranean-world/201808/22-tips-first-year-college-students.
2. Frank, Thomas. "42 College Tips I Learned Freshman Year." College Info Geek, March 4, 2011. https://collegeinfogeek.com/42-things-i-learned-freshman-year/.
3. Nicholas Provenzano, "Sharing with #Evernote at Conferences #ASCD13," The Nerdy Teacher, March 18, 2013, http://www.thenerdyteacher.com/2013/03/sharing-with-evernote-at-conferences.html.
4. Collins, Brandon. 2012. The 2 Hour Guide to Mastering Evernote - Including: Tips, Uses, and Evernote Essentials. 2nd ed. Future Prophet Publishing LLC.
5. Bert Webb, "14 Ways Evernote Can Help Principals Manage Schools," Open Loops, January 29, 2010, http://hwebbjr.typepad.com/openloops/2010/01/evernote-a-supervisors-digital-swiss-army-knife.html.
6. Ibid.

Appendix A: Search Operators

These search operators will help you find notes. These are the search operators I use most frequently. You can use them in combination. You can find a full list at https://help.evernote.com/hc/en-us/articles/208313828-Use-advanced-search-syntax

Notebook:
You could use the notebook operator rather than change notebooks if you want to restrict your search to a specific notebook. **Notebook:processed** will return results from the "processed" notebook only.

Tag:
Adding the tag operator will enable you to search through notes that have a specific tag. **tag:CAP** will return notes with the "CAP" tag.

If you want to use multiple tags, you will write the query as such:

tag:CAP tag:software_keys

-tag: - You would use the -tag operator if you want to see notes that do not have a specific tag. **-tag:CAP** will return all notes that do not have a "CAP" tag.

If you want to find all notes without a tag, search for **-tag:***

Created:
You can search through notes based on the date you created them. The format for the date must be YYYYMMDD. You can also search relative to the day.

created:20190311 will return notes created on March 11, 2019.

-created:20190311 will return notes created before March 11, 2019.

created:day will return notes created today.

created:week will return notes created this week (Sunday through Saturday).

created:month will return notes created this month.

created:year will return notes created this year.

-created:day will return notes created before today.

created:day-3 will return notes created in the last 3 days.

created:day-1 -created:day will return yesterday's notes.

created:month-1 -created:month will return last month's notes.

created:year-1 -created:year will return last year's notes.

created:20190101 -created:20190115 will show all notes between January 1, 2019, and January 15, 2019.

Todo:

The todo operator will return notes that have at least one checkbox.

todo:true will return all notes with at least one checkbox checked.

todo:false will return all notes with at least one checkbox that you have not checked.

todo:* will return all notes with at least a checkbox regardless if you checked it or not.

todo:false -todo:true will return notes that only have unchecked boxes.

Resource:

The resource operator lets you search for notes that have different file types associated with them. Here are resource types you can search for:

- image/gif

- image/jpeg

- image/png

- audio/wav

- audio/mpeg

- audio/amr

- application/pdf

- application/vnd.ms-excel

- application/vnd.ms-word

- application/vnd.ms-powerpoint

resource:application/PDF would result in notes with PDFs.

resource:audio/* will return notes with audio files.

-resource:image/* will return notes without images.

resource:application/vnd.ms-excel will return notes with a Microsoft Excel file.

Appendix B: Resources

Here is a list of useful tools I have referenced that integrate with Evernote. Please keep in mind that software and hardware come and go. I cannot guarantee that these tools will continue to remain available.

Bullet Journaling - Bullet journaling is a note taking strategy that Ryder Carroll developed. You can benefit from analog and digital note taking by scanning the pages into Evernote. You can learn more about bullet journaling through Ryder Carroll's website - https://bulletjournal.com/

Eidetic - Eidetic is a mobile application for spaced repitition learning. It integrates with Evernote. You can find it at http://www.eideticapp.com/

Hypothes.is - Hypothes.is is a social annotation application. You can highlight and annotate websites and PDF documents. Send the results to Evernote by using Hypothes.is in conjunction with Readwise.

IFTTT - "If This Than That" (IFTTT) is a web service that combines two applications to provide capabilities that otherwise would not exist. You can automate processes and send results automatically to Evernote. You can reach IFTTT at https://ifttt.com/

Penultimate - Penultimate is a digital note taking tool for iOs devices. You can handwrite notes and create sketches that you can then save to Evernote. You can find Penultimate on the Apple Store.

Readwise - You can import your highlights from Kindle, Hypothes.is, Instapaper, Pocket, iBooks, and many more apps. You can then review the notes you take on Readwise or have them exported to Evernote. You can find Readwise at https://readwise.io/

Reflect - Reflect is a flashcard application that uses spaced repitition to help you study. You can review your notes in the app, which draws from Evernote, or receive a daily review email. You can learn more at https://www.reflectapp.io/

ScanSnap - ScanSnap is a document scanner. It will scan a stack of documents in seconds as a PDF document to Evernote. Search for ScanSnap iX1500.

Bibliography

Adam. "My Tribute to Evernote: A Student's Guide." *The Flannelboard* (blog), March 24, 2012. http://theflannelboard.blogspot.com/2012/03/my-tribute-to-evernote-students-guide.html.

Alhinty, Mona. "English-Language Learning at Their Fingertips." *International Journal of Mobile and Blended Learning* 7, no. 2 (January 1, 2015): 45–63. https://doi.org/10.4018/ijmbl.2015040104.

Betts, Jennifer. "Actionable Long-Term Goal Examples for College Students." Accessed November 26, 2021. https://examples.yourdictionary.com/actionable-long-term-goal-examples-for-college-students.html.

Clear, James. *Atomic Habits: Tiny Changes, Remarkable Results: An Easy & Proven Way to Build Good Habits & Break Bad Ones*. New York: Avery, an imprint of Penguin Random House, 2018.

ClydeBank Technology. *Evernote: Mastery - Exactly How To Use Evernote To Organize Your Life, Manage Your Day & Get Things Done (Evernote, Evernote Essentials, Evernote Mastery, Evernote For Dummies, Time Management)*. ClydeBank Media LLC, 2014. http://www.amazon.com/dp/B00MLQ4MT6/ref=r_soa_w_d.

Collier, Jordan. "19 Practical Evernote Ideas Students Can Begin Using Today," 2012. https://evernoteforstudents.files.wordpress.com/2012/09/19-practical-evernote-ideas1.pdf.

Collins, Brandon. *The 2 Hour Guide to Mastering Evernote - Including: Tips, Uses, and Evernote Essentials.* 2nd ed. Future Prophet Publishing LLC, 2012.

Copeland, Philip. "Evernote for Every Choir, Composer, Classroom, and Conductor." *Choral Journal* 56, no. 1 (August 1, 2015): 49–54.

Crystal. "Mastering MOOCs with Evernote." Personal Knowledge Management for Academia & Librarians, October 20, 2014. http://www.academicpkm.org/2014/10/20/mastering-moocs-evernote/.

DeSchryver, Michael. "Web-Mediated Knowledge Synthesis for Educators." *Journal of Adolescent & Adult Literacy* 58, no. 5 (February 1, 2015): 388–96. https://doi.org/10.1002/jaal.373.

Donaldson, David, and Joe Allen. *Getting Things Done the David Allen Way with Evernote: A Beginner's Guidebook on How to Master GTD with Evernote,* n.d.

Doubek, James. "Attention, Students: Put Your Laptops Away." NPR.org, April 17, 2016. https://www.npr.org/2016/04/17/474525392/attention-students-put-your-laptops-away.

Elisabeth. "How Academics Use Evernote to Make Life Easier." Personal Knowledge Management for Academia & Librarians, July 30, 2013. http://www.academicpkm.org/2013/07/30/how-exactly-do-people-use-evernote-in-academia/.

Evernote Blog. "5 Tips to Use Evernote For Academic Achievement," April 14, 2014. http://blog.evernote.com/blog/2014/04/14/5-tips-use-evernote-academic-achievement/.

Evernote Blog. "10 Tips for Using Evernote to De-Stress College from Student Ambassador Megan Cotter," April 18, 2012. https://blog.evernote.com/blog/2012/04/18/10-tips-for-using-evernote-to-de-stress-college-from-student-ambassador-megan-cotter/.

Evernote Blog. "How Evernote Can Help You Achieve Your Goals | Evernote." *Evernote.Com | Blog* (blog), December 29, 2014. https://evernote.com/blog/how-evernote-can-help-you-achieve-your-goals/.

Frank, Thomas. "42 College Tips I Learned Freshman Year." *College Info Geek* (blog), March 4, 2011. https://collegeinfogeek.com/42-things-i-learned-freshman-year/.

GearFire - Tips for Students. "Using Evernote to Save Your Schooling." Accessed October 13, 2017. http://www.gearfire.net/evernote-school/.

Geher, Glenn. "22 Tips for First-Year College Students." *Psychology Today* (blog), August 9, 2018. https://www.psychologytoday.com/blog/darwins-subterranean-world/201808/22-tips-first-year-college-students.

Hansen, Randall. "25 Tips to Help You Survive and Thrive Your Freshman Year." LiveCareer, December 15, 2017. https://www.livecareer.com/resources/jobs/search/first-year-success.

Hunt, Joy Suzanne. "How to Use Evernote to Organize Research." *The Cafe Scholar* (blog), July 24, 2017. https://www.thecafescholar.com/use-evernote-organize-research/.

Hyatt, Michael. "A Better Filing System for Public Speakers (and Writers)." *Michael Hyatt & Co.* (blog), February 18, 2011. https://michaelhyatt.com/how-to-use-evernote-if-you-are-a-speaker-or-writer.html.

Hyatt, Michael S. *Free to Focus: A Total Productivity System to Achieve More by Doing Less*. Grand Rapids, Michigan: Baker Book, a division of Baker Publishing Group, 2019.

Indiana Jen. "Using Evernote for Research," February 28, 2013. https://indianajen.com/2013/02/28/using-evernote-for-research/.

Kowalczyk, Piotr. "8 Evernote Tips for Book Lovers." *Ebook Friendly* (blog), May 15, 2014. http://ebookfriendly.com/evernote-tips-for-booklovers/.

Milligan, Jonathan. "A Simple Guide to Indexing the Books You Read for Evernote." *JonathanMilligan.Com* (blog), June 4, 2014. http://jonathanmilligan.com/a-simple-guide-to-indexing-the-books-you-read-for-evernote/.

Mitchell, Travis, and Emma Kerr. "12 Ways to Prepare for Your Freshman Year of College." U.S. News & World Report, June 29, 2020. https://www.usnews.com/education/best-colleges/slideshows/10-ways-to-prepare-for-your-freshman-year-of-college.

National Society of High School Scholars. "How to Survive Freshman Year of College," July 6, 2018. https://www.nshss.org/blog/how-to-survive-freshman-year-of-college/.

Pascarella, Alyssa. "12 Tips to Help You Survive Your Freshman Year of College." *RISLA - RI Student Loan Authority* (blog), August 11, 2017. https://blog.risla.com/how-to-survive-your-freshman-year-of-college.

Peterson, Deb. "Why You Should Write Practice Tests While You Study." ThoughtCo, May 30, 2019. https://www.thoughtco.com/make-practice-tests-while-you-study-31622.

Pipes, Taylor. "Taking Note: What Commonplace Books Can Teach Us about Our Past." *Evernote Blog* (blog), February 26, 2016. https://blog.evernote.com/blog/2016/02/26/taking-note-what-commonplace-books-can-teach-us-about-our-past/.

Price, S., C. Jewitt, and M. Sakr. "Embodied Experiences of Place: A Study of History Learning with Mobile Technologies." *Journal of Computer Assisted Learning* 32, no. 4 (August 1, 2016): 345. https://doi.org/10.1111/jcal.12137.

Provenzano, Nicholas. "Sharing with #Evernote at Conferences #ASCD13." *The Nerdy Teacher* (blog), March 18, 2013. http://www.thenerdyteacher.com/2013/03/sharing-with-evernote-at-conferences.html.

Samuel, Alexandra. *Work Smarter with Evernote*. Harvard Business School Publishing Corporation, 2013.

Seideman, Melissa. "Part 2: Evernote for the Social Studies." *Not Another History Teacher* (blog), September 14, 2012. http://notanotherhistoryteacher.edublogs.org/2012/09/14/part-2-evernote-for-the-social-studies/.

Sinkov, Andrew. "Emailing Into Evernote Just Got Better." *Evernote Blog* (blog), March 16, 2010. https://blog.evernote.com/blog/2010/03/16/emailing-into-evernote-just-got-better/.

Stachowiak, Bonni Jean. *The Productive Online and Offline Professor: A Practical Guide*. First edition. Thrive Online Series. Sterling, Virginia: Stylus Publishing, 2020.

The Brain that Wouldn't Die. "Evernote: A Guide for Academics." Accessed October 13, 2017. https://brainthatwouldntdie.wordpress.com/2013/09/30/evernote-a-guide-for-academics/.

Van Dyke, Aaron R., and Jillian Smith-Carpenter. "Bring Your Own Device: A Digital Notebook for Undergraduate Biochemistry Laboratory Using a Free, Cross-Platform Application." *Journal of Chemical Education* 94, no. 5 (May 1, 2017): 656.

Walsh, Emily, and Ilseung Cho. "Using Evernote as an Electronic Lab Notebook in a Translational Science Laboratory." *Journal of Laboratory Automation* 18, no. 3 (June 1, 2013): 229–34. https://doi.org/10.1177/2211068212471834.

Ward, David. *Evernote for Lawyers: A Guide to Getting Organized & Increasing Productivity*. The Attorney Marketing Center, n.d.

Webb, Bert. "14 Ways Evernote Can Help Principals Manage Schools." *Open Loops* (blog), January 29, 2010. http://hwebbjr.typepad.com/openloops/2010/01/evernote-a-supervisors-digital-swiss-army-knife.html.

About the Author

Stan Skrabut is a card-carrying lifelong learner who has spent his career helping people and organizations achieve improved performance. He is a scholar, teacher, author, veteran, martial artist, and avid reader. Throughout his working life, he has changed roles and responsibilities countless times. He worked as a guard, organizational trainer, instructional technologist, webmaster, systems programmer, lecturer, and director. He uses informal learning, especially reading, as a way to improve himself and subsequently his teams. His interest in informal learning inspired his dissertation topic, *Study of Informal Learning Among University of Wyoming Extension Educators.*

He lives with his wife and two dogs in Rhode Island. Nomadic in nature, he loves to travel and has lived in Germany, Belgium, Holland, Turkey, and various locations across the United States. His number one passion is helping others achieve their goals.

Also By

Read to Succeed: The Power of Books to Transform Your Life and Put You on the Path to Success by Stan Skrabut

In *Read to Succeed* learn that there are countless benefits to reading including idea generation, longevity, and increased mental functions among many others. Developing a reading habit that will open you up to new ideas is easy to start and by reading this book, you will learn how to develop a reading habit that will last.

The book recounts the reading habits of our Founding Fathers. In addition, it shares the reading plans of well-known successful business leaders such as Bill Gates, Warren Buffet, and Oprah Winfrey. These pillars of our society all have similar reading habits. This book uses its strategies to help anyone become a more effective reader. Further, this book lays out realistic ideas on how to incorporate reading into your personal game plan to succeed and accomplish your goals. Whether you are a beginning college student or already on your way to success in the professional world, this book has something for you to hasten your path. Start building a reading habit right away!

Printed in Great Britain
by Amazon

86596643R00095